Child Sex, Bacha Bazi and Prost

Musa Khan Jalalzai

Child Sex, Bacha Bazi and Prostitution in Afghanistan

Male Prostitution, Forced Marriages, Play Boy, Women, Arms and Drug Trafficking.

LAP LAMBERT Academic Publishing

Impressum/Imprint (nur für Deutschland/only for Germany)
Bibliografische Information der Deutschen Nationalbibliothek: Die Deutsche Nationalbibliothek verzeichnet diese Publikation in der Deutschen Nationalbibliografie; detaillierte bibliografische Daten sind im Internet über http://dnb.d-nb.de abrufbar.
Alle in diesem Buch genannten Marken und Produktnamen unterliegen warenzeichen-, marken- oder patentrechtlichem Schutz bzw. sind Warenzeichen oder eingetragene Warenzeichen der jeweiligen Inhaber. Die Wiedergabe von Marken, Produktnamen, Gebrauchsnamen, Handelsnamen, Warenbezeichnungen u.s.w. in diesem Werk berechtigt auch ohne besondere Kennzeichnung nicht zu der Annahme, dass solche Namen im Sinne der Warenzeichen- und Markenschutzgesetzgebung als frei zu betrachten wären und daher von jedermann benutzt werden dürften.

Coverbild: www.ingimage.com

Verlag: LAP LAMBERT Academic Publishing GmbH & Co. KG
Dudweiler Landstr. 99, 66123 Saarbrücken, Deutschland
Telefon +49 681 3720-310, Telefax +49 681 3720-3109
Email: info@lap-publishing.com

Herstellung in Deutschland:
Schaltungsdienst Lange o.H.G., Berlin
Books on Demand GmbH, Norderstedt
Reha GmbH, Saarbrücken
Amazon Distribution GmbH, Leipzig
ISBN: 978-3-8454-7361-1

Imprint (only for USA, GB)
Bibliographic information published by the Deutsche Nationalbibliothek: The Deutsche Nationalbibliothek lists this publication in the Deutsche Nationalbibliografie; detailed bibliographic data are available in the Internet at http://dnb.d-nb.de.
Any brand names and product names mentioned in this book are subject to trademark, brand or patent protection and are trademarks or registered trademarks of their respective holders. The use of brand names, product names, common names, trade names, product descriptions etc. even without a particular marking in this works is in no way to be construed to mean that such names may be regarded as unrestricted in respect of trademark and brand protection legislation and could thus be used by anyone.

Cover image: www.ingimage.com

Publisher: LAP LAMBERT Academic Publishing GmbH & Co. KG
Dudweiler Landstr. 99, 66123 Saarbrücken, Germany
Phone +49 681 3720-310, Fax +49 681 3720-3109
Email: info@lap-publishing.com

Printed in the U.S.A.
Printed in the U.K. by (see last page)
ISBN: 978-3-8454-7361-1

CONTENTS

1

FOREWARD

Every month, hundreds of Afghan children, women and unemployed young men are kidnapped, imprisoned or trafficked to international market and local prostitution industry. In Pakistan and Afghanistan, war criminals have left a shameful record of child sex, children trafficking, kidnapping and play boy business. In Northern Afghanistan and parts of North-western Pakistan, majority of orphan, poor and maroon children became the victim of these sex hungry beasts who not only abuse them but share them with friends as well.

Prostitution in Afghanistan is in increase that every month, four male and female enters prostitution. Kabul shur Bazaar, Lahori Gate, Sarai Ghazni, Karthi Seh, Khyr Khana, Deh Mazang and some other places is fast becoming a hub for male prostitution. One can find dozens of male 'prostitutes', who mainly are in the age group of 15 to 30 years, waiting for customers in these busy places, but not everyone can identify these men selling 'unnatural' sex.

Despite the fact that the phenomenon is increasing by the minute, no government body or NGO has conducted a survey to find out exactly how many men are in this business. People are also as blissfully ignorant of the diseases that male prostitution contributes to the society.

Social and political conditions in Afghanistan are complex and profoundly oppressive. The question is, whether abolition of prostitution is the answer for the thousands of women living in Poverty, or this business is the sole source of employment? The answer is no because there is no alternative source of life for these people.

Male and female prostitution in Afghanistan is shrouded in mystery. Due to the fear of the Taliban and extremist mullahs, male and female prostitutes cannot introduce themselves as prostitutes. They sexual trends in Afghanistan are strong or thousands men and women are involved in the industry, but these people live in fear.

The law treats woman as a victim, and the pimps and customers face a possibility of a death sentence. Prostitution is not limited to girls and women, Government officials and social scientists believe that there is fast increase in homosexuality in the country. There are cultural and socioeconomic factors or practices that encourage or lead to prostitution. Once a male prostitute in Kabul told me:

"In the city, the boys' clients are tabled as men who have sex with men (including men who don't identify as gay); sugar mummies and daddies; wives of male clients and visitors."Many closet homosexuals in conjugal situations employ masseurs for sexual gratification," said Jamal Khan Saeedi.

Jamal Khan was talking about the idiosyncrasies of some of his women-customers, most of who belong to the affluent class. One customer, the wife of a rich Afghan parliamentarian, took him to her bedroom and asked him to just keep looking at her for the whole night. Another woman, wife of an Afghan cleric told him that she was sex hungry since long time as her husband was involved with a play boy. She never got satisfaction because her husband was male lover.

She of course paid him his full charges and also tipped him over and above that. Jamal Khan was in nice mood and said that: *some times women of rich families ask him to give a massage for her aching limbs for the whole night. Some ask him to just go on kissing her all night long"*.

"I am very sad and life these days has become so fast that my husband does not have time for sex me properly, I am thirsty and sex hungry, a wife an Afghan politician told him. Growing poverty, increasing urbanization, widespread unemployment, and breaking up of joint family system etc, are responsible factors for the prevalence and perpetuation of male and female prostitution. Child prostitutes become ready recruits for flesh trade for they are rendered unfit for any other trade or calling not being educated or having any knowledge of any other trade.

With the transfer of power to the Afghan army, drug-lords and warlords in Afghanistan, the import and export of children and women is likely to boost as the state drivers have a good experience in this business. In RAWA website, Heidi Kingston reported some important cases of brutalities against women. Heidi reported the selling of women in an open market in Shinwari district of Jalalabad province.

"Big chadors cover their heads and just the women's hands show. Like animals they are bought and sold." according to Afghanistan Independent Human Rights Commission report. *"Two women were sold with their children and one woman was sold to five different people and returned back to the original man who sold her, then killed her"*. AIHRC reported.

The sold women are kept in lock up, raped again and again and then killed. The police and judiciary have not launched any formal investigations to determine the causes and motivations of suicide and self-burning by women. AIHRC and RAWA reported a 14-year-old Afghan girl, Samia, victim of gang-rape by warlords in Sar-e-Pul province in Northern Afghanistan. She told an Afghan TV Channel that warlords not only raped her but imprisoned her father and brother when they publicized the issue and asked for justice.

This is not a single case, one of my friends from Jalal Ahmad once told me that in Mazar, and a Tajik warlord not only raped a 15 years girl but killed her father as well.

The story of Shafiqa is not too different. She was married to a Tajik warlord family where she was treated as a slave, beaten with electric cables, stoned, her limbs broken with an axe handle and doused with boiling water. She told reporters that her father-in-law tortured her further by literally rubbing salt into her wounds. Amnesty International report has quoted some incidents of the massacre of innocent women in their homes by war criminals.

In Northern Afghanistan, scores of young women have been kidnapped and then raped. Hundreds of raped women committed suicide or killed by their relatives. Thousands maroon and poor women and girls have disappeared and several have been stoned to death.

The three decades long brutal civil war, foreign interventions, poverty, unemployment, militarization, ignorance, warlordism, regionalism, knife and gun culture and political rivalries are factors making the women and children of Afghanistan vulnerable to trafficking, prostitution and play boy business.

Afghanistan shares borders with Iran, Pakistan, China and Central Asian States and offers an environment for facilitating the business of women, children and drug trafficking. Over one hundred male and female prostitution centres are in operation in the capital Kabul. These prostitution centres receive protection from the police, politicians, parliamentarians and higher government officials.

A heart-breaking story of an Afghan girl who was sold again and again in the hands of criminal mafia groups is indicative of the increasing violence against women. A young girl of poor parents, Benazir was twelve years old when she was forcefully married to an illiterate man. She remained with him for nine years and had four children. After nine years, her husband sold her to a human trafficker.

The trafficker sold to another man in Northern Afghanistan. He kept her for a month, and sold to another man, two month later she was sold to a fourth man and after a year she was resold to a criminal.

What happened to Benazir, nobody knows but Benazir is not the only victim of war criminals in her country, there are thousands women and girls in Afghanistan whose life is in danger. Cases of rape are in thousands, torture and domestic violence in Northern Afghanistan is being encouraged by mafia groups.

Recently, in Balkh Province, a teenager girl was kidnapped, tortured and raped by a warlord. This was a great shame for her family. Her parent decided to kill her but a local NGO saved her life. Brothels in Mazar-e-Sharif, Balkh, Laghman, Samangan and Kundoz provinces openly campaign for young girls.

As they have strong support from the war criminal partners and corrupt officials in the police department, they are freely run their businesses. Neither have they taught people about HIV virus nor about AIDs. Consequently, over one hundred thousand people are suffering from HIV virus in Afghanistan.

Women and girls who wish to contest the legality of their marriages face both social and legal obstacles. Girls who approach the police seeking to escape from forced or child marriage can find themselves arrested for having "run away from home," although this is not a crime under Afghan criminal law or sharia. Local police and prosecutors often display limited awareness of Afghan law, and instead enforce the norms of customary law or traditions.

In rural areas, selling of women and children and debt bondage businesses are growing, but are often disguised as marriage. Extreme poverty, ignorance and warlordism are among the problems which have pushed many minors - boys and girls - into situations of peonage. Some poor parents often offer their young daughters as loan brides. Recently, in Herat province, more than 150 cases of the selling of children, especially girls, were reported.

Afghanistan's Independent Human Rights Commission recently voiced about the surge in women and child trafficking in the country. In its latest report, AIHRC has warned that: "human traffickers used coordinated methods to allure women and children to take them outside the country.

Poverty, unemployment, corruption and insecurity are the factors behind an increase in human trafficking. After women and children are trafficked out of the country, they get sexually abused and face other sorts of violence."

The US State Department in its report on trafficking in persons for 2010 has revealed that trafficking of human being in Afghanistan is more prevalent than transnational trafficking, and the majority of victims are children.

Poor and unemployed Afghan children are being trafficked within the country and sent to male prostitution centres. Business of forced begging is controlled by these mafia groups within and outside the government circles. Begging is considered to be the most profitable industry in Afghanistan that finances insurgency, ethnicity and weapon industry.

In all 34 provinces of the country, thousands men, women and children are begging on behalf of underground mafia groups. Organized and professional criminal gangs in big cities collect million in Afghan currency from across the country and share it with their friend within the government departments.

The begging women perform two jobs; prostitution and fund raising. Young girls visit the houses of dignitaries, parliamentarians, police officers, army generals and foreign contractors.

A US report warns that some Afghan families willingly sell their young children in prostitution, including Bacha Bazi and dancing clubs. The US human trafficking report has revealed that: "brothels and prostitution rings are sometimes run by foreigners, sometimes with links to larger criminal networks. Tajik women are also believed to be trafficked through Afghanistan to other countries for prostitution. Trafficked Iranian women transit Afghanistan en route to Pakistan."

As Daily outlook editorial 26-7-2011) painted an ugly picture of the state of women and girls in the country: *"Women and children are the easiest victims to human trafficking. The societies marked with disorder, economic instability and deteriorated law and order situation mostly suffer from the problem of human trafficking".*

According to the latest report of Afghanistan Independent Human Rights Commission (AIHRC) the poverty stricken people whose hopelessness have doubled with the consistent insecurity, some way or the other, become victims and they are trafficked to different parts of the country and even in the neighbouring countries where they are tested by further misery.

There have been many occasions when wives are trafficked and pushed to prostitution by their own husbands and daughters by their own parents. The children who are orphan are further closer to the possibility of being the victims."

In Monthly Cutting Edge, Nick Schwellenbach and Carol D. Leonnig (July 26th 2010) have painted another painful story about the involvement of US contractors in sex trafficking in Bosnia, Afghanistan and Iraq: *"Nearly a decade after DynCorp International LLC employees were implicated in Bosnia for buying and selling women from throughout Eastern Europe — and not prosecuted — the U.S. Army was told this February that supervisors of an Army subcontractor in Iraq had sexually assaulted women who were held in involuntary servitude."*

On the involvement of US contractors in child sex in Afghanistan, Joseph Farah's G2 Bulletin has reported a US military contractor's involvement in child sex (Bacha Bazi) who dressed up young boys in woman dress so as to present for dance in a party and potentially to be sold for sex. All these diseases are fuelled by drug addiction across the country.

In post Taliban Afghanistan, no woman is secure as the new family law badly affected women rights. According to the new family law, a husband must provide all necessities to his wife. But it also says that he can withhold this support if she refuses to "submit to her husband's reasonable sexual enjoyment,"

There are many communities living in Afghanistan but nobody wants to support this law. Bisexual gay, lesbian, and transgender are living in fear. Homosexuality and cross-dressing are not considered serious crimes in Afghanistan, dancing boys change dresses, involve in homosexuality.

During the Taliban regime, homosexuality, play boy and Bach Bazi (sodomy) was openly in practice. Every Mullah had his own boy in his house away from his village. After 9/11, Afghan bisexuals and gay got more freedom and involved in sexual relations with foreign forces. Some Afghan gays who received serious threats claimed asylum in both UK and USA.

But many accuse the Taliban of hypocrisy on the issue of homosexuality. The Taliban had boys but they kept it secret, they hid their boys in their madrasas. Among the Pashtuns women are considered inferior, unclean and unworthy of male attention except to reproduce.

Local farmers, adult students and middle-aged Afghan have now become addicted in Northern Afghanistan. A British soldier recently returned home from Afghanistan has described a shameful story of Bacha Bazi in Afghanistan:

"They were more terrifying than the al-Qaeda. One bloke who had painted toenails was offering to paint ours. They go about hand in hand, mincing around the village." While the marines failed to find any al-Qaeda during the seven-day Operation Condor, they were propositioned by dozens of men in villages the troops were ordered to search. "We were pretty shocked," Marine Fletcher said. "We discovered from the Afghan soldiers we had with us that a lot of men in this country have the same philosophy as ancient Greeks: 'a woman for babies, a man for pleasure'."

Warlord's militias are deeply involved in sexual relations with boys. In 1994, the Taliban, were called to rescue a boy over whom two commanders had fought. A Mazar-e-Sharif man once told me that: *"If you want a boy for sex, 'you need to follow him before he will agree".* This tradition now becomes a custom in Hazaras of Northern Afghanistan. A UK based Persian speaking Afghan once told me that he had three boys and a wife in Afghanistan and treated them equally.

Peter Foster of Sunday Morning Herald reported (October 7, 2005) an Afghan who faced death penalty when fell in love with and "married" a 16-year-old boy. *The "marriage" between Liaquat Ali, 42, and a teenager, Markeen, was conducted with all the ceremony of a conventional tribal wedding, including a troupe of singers and a feast."* The newspaper reported. According to journalist Najeebullah Qureshi, an Afghan commander once told him:

"I had a boy because every commander had a partner."Among the commanders there is competition, and if I didn't have one, then I could not compete with them." "I go to every province to have happiness and pleasure with boys," says an Afghan man known as "The German," who acts as a bacha bazi pimp, supplying boys to the men. "Some boys are not good for dancing, and they will be used for other purposes.... I mean for sodomy and other sexual activities."

As Wiki Leaks revealed high-ranking Afghan officials quashing reports of police officers and other Afghans arrested for "purchasing a service from a child." The involvement of Afghan army and police in male prostitution is not new. American soldiers refused to work with Afghan homosexual army soldiers when he was sexually harassed. "It's not about homosexuality as much as it is about the young boys. Some of the Afghans have their own young boys they use for sexual purposes and we can't do anything about it, they complained.

Musa Khan Jalalzai.
August—2011. London.

CHAPTER ONE

PLAY BOY, FORCED MARRIAGES AND PROSTITUTION IN AFGHANISTAN

The heart breaking stories of helpless, poor and vulnerable girls, boys and women of Afghanistan are making headlines in print and electronic media across Europe, Pakistan and Afghanistan. Afghan women and young boys continue to be victim of domestic and sexual violence by warlords, war criminals and private militia commanders. Women and girls are kidnapped, raped and sold to prostitution in Northern Afghanistan.

During the last three years, I have been receiving e-mails from some helpless Afghan women and children about their heart breaking stories of forced marriages, massacre in their homes, or have brutally beaten and raped by war criminals and Afghan police officials.

All e-mails I received are more painful and heartbreaking. Some girls wrote to me about their helplessness, some wrote their rape stories and some say they have been raped again and again and finally sold into the hands of war criminals that treat then like animals. Women in Afghan jails have mostly been victim of rape and torture.

In all Afghan jails, women prisoners are abused, vilified, raped, presented in official parties and keep as slaves. Young teenagers sleep with police officials, they are raped all the night on the pretext that they would be released very soon if they continue serving sex hungry officials. There are hundred thousands secret stories about the women prisoners who got pregnant in various Afghan jails. Abortion rate in the country is very high. Hundred thousands young women kill their babies every year.

The Frontier Post reported (August 4, 1995) scores of young women have been abducted and then raped, taken as wives by religious extremist criminals or sold into local

10

prostitution. *"Some have committed suicide to avoid such a fate. Scores of women have reportedly "disappeared" and several have been stoned to death".* Hundreds of thousands of women and children have been displaced or are living as refugees abroad.

Young girls are in danger from sex hungry criminals while young boys are more vulnerable as they are forcefully taken to dancing clubs. Many are traumatized by the horrific abuses they have suffered or witnessed. In their e-mails letters, they complain that rape is not considered as a serious crime in the country, if a woman reports a rape case to the police investigation began about her character. The network of prostitution has recently developed across Northern Afghanistan.

In one of the e-mails I received from Takhar province described the story of two small girls and a woman raped by armed men in 15 June 2011. A six-year old girl was also among the victims. However, a 15-year-old girl was gang-raped by five armed men of a Tajik warlord in Kalifgan district.

Afghan Human rights official told Pajhwok news that more than 2,765 cases of violence against women and girls were reported to the rights watchdog while Fawzia Amini, of the Afghan Ministry of Women's Affairs revealed that some 6,765 cases of violence against women and girls were registered in 2010.

Despite Afghanistan's law requiring a minimum age for marriage and the provision of consent, the majority of brides are under the legal minimum age and many marriages are forced. According to UNIFEM and Human Rights Watch, more than 70 percent of marriages were forced in 2009 and 2010. Most marriages are arranged by parents and other family members. Opulent, warlords and drug traffickers keep three to five wives.

Except in some urban areas of Afghanistan, the majority of young men and women do not choose their own spouses. The practice of giving women to another family to settle disputes or debts is common today, though legally prohibited by a presidential decree. Women are frequently abused or confined at home for refusing their family's choice of marriage partner or attempting to run away from a forced marriage.

The three decades long brutal civil war, foreign interventions, poverty, unemployment, militarization, ignorance, warlordism, regionalism, knife and gun culture and political rivalries are factors making the women and children of Afghanistan vulnerable to trafficking, prostitution and play boy business.

Afghanistan shares borders with Iran, Pakistan, China and Central Asian States and offers an environment for facilitating the business of women, children and drug trafficking. Over one hundred male and female prostitution centres are in operation in the capital Kabul. These prostitution centres are protected by the police, politicians, parliamentarians and higher government officials.

Women and girls who wish to contest the legality of their marriages face both social and legal obstacles. Girls who approach the police seeking to escape from forced or child marriage can find themselves arrested for having "run away from home," although this is not a crime under Afghan criminal law or Sharia. Local police and prosecutors often display limited awareness of Afghan law, and instead enforce the norms of customary law or traditions.

The Afghanistan Law of Marriages (1971) stipulates that a legal marriage must be two Muslim adults of the opposite sex, and that it must meet the rules of Islamic law. While the law does not explicitly address the issue of same-sex couples, Article 41 of the Marriage Law stipulates that where the law is silent on a particular issue, it shall be decided based on the principles of Islamic law.

Afghanistan's post-Taliban constitution enshrines equal rights for women, but in practice, discrimination is still rife. Activists alleged Karzai enacted the controversial family law to appease conservative Shia clergy ahead of presidential election. The new law includes a section saying that a husband must provide financially for his wife.

But it also says that he can withhold this support if she refuses to "submit to her husband's reasonable sexual enjoyment," according to a translation of the article supplied by New York-based Human Rights Watch.

In Kabul between 100 and 200 women protested the Shia Family Law and were met by a mob of 800 counterdemonstrators who were mainly men and Shia clergy. Many women were prevented from attending the protest by male family members and were denied entry to board buses by public transportation employees.

The Shia Family Law was passed in 2009 for the 3 to 6 million Shia Muslims who reside in Afghanistan. Under the law, women must not refuse the husband's sexual demands, women must comply to intercourse every four days unless sick, women may not gain employment or receive education without their husband's permission, wives leaving home must do so with male escort or with permission and they must dress up and wear cosmetics according to the husband's desires.

Refusal to do any of these would be illegal for the woman and can be enforced — the husband may stop feeding her. "If a woman says no, the man has the right not to feed her," said Ayatollah Mohammed Asif Mohseni.

Some female politicians decided to take more pragmatic stance on the original proposed marriage age of girls from nine to 16 and removing completely provisions for temporary marriages. In Afghanistan, where most women are uneducated and depend on their husbands for food and clothing.

The legislation was passed by presidential decree in mid-July and published in Afghanistan's official gazette on July 27, which brings the law into force, according to Human Rights Watch. Lawmakers confirmed the process. Shinkai Kharokhel, a lawmaker who has been involved in reforming the legislation, said no one from the administration told her that the law was being approved without further debate. Instead, she learned third hand that the law she had been fighting was now in effect.

The United Nations Development Fund for Women said that the law "legalizes the rape of a wife by her husband." Robert Wood, a State Department spokesman, said that the United States was "very concerned" about the law. "We urge President Karzai to review the law's legal status to correct provisions of the law that limit or restrict women's rights," he said.

I really wish this hadn't been made into a Rape Issue. Yes, the sanction of spousal rape is implied by the law, according to very reliable sources, but there are other problematic things about the law, such as restrictions on women's freedom of movement and rights to education, work and access to healthcare.

Hamid Karzai was accused for trying to win votes in Afghanistan's presidential election by backing a law the UN said legalises rape within marriage and bans wives from stepping outside their homes without their husbands' permission. The Afghan president signed the law, despite condemnation by human rights activists and some MPs that it flouts the constitution's equal rights provisions.

The final document has not been published, but the law is believed to contain articles that rule women cannot leave the house without their husbands' permission, that they can only seek work, education or visit the doctor with their husbands' permission, and that they cannot refuse their husband sex. A briefing document prepared by the United Nations Development Fund for Women also warns that the law grants custody of children to fathers and grandfathers only.

Majority of Afghan children, women and girls trafficked in and outside the country are being sold in the local prostitution markets or in the hands of wealthy individuals, warlords and private militia commanders. UNICEF in its report revealed that fifty seven percent of Afghan marriages involve girls under sixteen. Insecurity, fear of kidnapping and rape has also prompted many families to force their young daughters into marriage.

In Northern Afghanistan, and in parts of Southern provinces, the same story is repeated. In various districts of Northern provinces, poor and poverty stricken girls and children are being kidnapped and sold into prostitution. Unemployed and poor young boys have also been subjected to trafficking for male prostitution, forced labour and play boy business.

The traditions of child marriage have long been practiced in Afghanistan. Afghanistan's civil war left hundred of thousands women widow and young children orphaned. As matrimonial life is much expensive across the country, specifically, in Paktika and Paktia provinces, the price for a young girl has been fixed more than three millions in Afghan currency.

Education for girls in these provinces is considered to be a great sin while sports and other hobbies are not allowed. Majority of Afghan girls became pregnant before they reach physical maturity because they don't know about the family law of the country. The Afghan Civil Law sets the minimum age for marriage at sixteen for girls and at eighteen for boys.

A heart-breaking story of an Afghan girl who was sold again and again in the hands of criminal mafia groups is indicative of the increasing violence against women. A young girl of poor parents, Benazir was twelve years old when she was forcefully married to an illiterate man. She remained with him for nine years and had four children. After nine years, her husband sold her to a human trafficker.

He kept her for a month, and sold to another man, two month later she was sold to a fourth man and after a year she was resold to a criminal. What happened to Benazir, nobody knows but Benazir is not the only victim of war criminals in her country, there are thousands women and girls in Afghanistan whose life is in danger. Cases of rape are in thousands, torture and domestic violence in Northern Afghanistan is being encouraged by mafia groups.

Recently, in Balkh Province, a teenager girl was kidnapped, tortured and raped by a warlord. This was a great shame for her family. Her parent decided to kill her but a local NGO saved her life. Brothels in Mazar-e-Sharif, Balkh, Laghman, Samangan and Kundoz provinces openly campaign for young girls.

As they have strong support from the war criminal partners and corrupt officials in the police department, they are freely run their businesses. Neither have they taught people about HIV virus nor about AIDs. Consequently, over one hundred thousand people are suffering from HIV virus in Afghanistan.

Another profitable business which has attracted thousands criminal elements and warlords is, playing with boys or "having sex with boys". This is an old and ugly tradition of Afghanistan. Orphan and poor children are picked from the streets or purchased from their parents who agree to sell them to those wealthy males who are fond of homosexuality. The parents are normally agreed on a "good price" for their child.

This is neither illegal in Afghanistan nor the police show any interest to intercept it. In Kandahar, and parts of Northern Afghanistan, Afghan married and unmarried men love boys roughly 15 to 20 years old. The price of a young and beautiful boy has been fixed up to 100,000 Afghanis.

"Keeping a beautiful boy has become a custom in Kandahar now," a Kandahari homosexual once told me. When we study the poetry books in Kandahar or in any province in the North, we come across many poems about homosexuality.

Male prostitution has not been considered a harmful business in Afghanistan since decades. Though, keeping a play boy or Bacha Bereesh (a boy without beard) is not illegal but thousands wealthy people, business men and criminal gangs are involved with play boys across the country since long. After the US invasion in 2001, sex trafficking in the country becomes a profitable business.

One of my police friends recently told me that more than 3000 families in Jowzjan, Mazar, Kundoz, Herat, Samangan and Faryab provinces have been involved in prostitution since last ten years. The main factor behind this business he told me is poverty and unemployment.

Here, I want to quote some Afghan male prostitutes and gays from various websites to find out how they are looking for their desired boys or adult male:

MundoAnuncio.com / Kabul. Clasificados gratis - Compra venta y servicios

1--I am looking for boys under r 20 years old for fun and Sex and kissing romance - Kabul - Kabul

2--My name is Aryan and seeking boys. Seeking: I am looking for boys under r 20 years old for fun and sex and kissing romance. I am gay, 26 years.

3--I am 25 years old and I am body builder, contact with Aryan: I am looking for boys under 20 years old for fun and Sex and kissing romance – Kabul. Gay Afghanistan. Gay Kabul

4--I Like guy Sex to guy. if u Want contact me 0093775467704 - Kabul – Kabul. My name is saleem and seeking gay, seeking: I like guy sex to guy .if u want contact me 0093775467704.

5--I an m gay, 23 years. I like sex and kissing so much 0775467704. Contact with saleem: I Like guy Sex to guy. if u Want contact me 0093775467704 - Kabul

6--I Want a Nice Gay seeking gay - Kapisa – Kapisa Afghanistan. My name is olgun and seeking gay

7--Seeking: I want a nice gay seeking gay. I am gay, 41 years

8--I want to be sex.gay sex, boy sex, women sex, transex...contact with olgun: I Want a Nice Gay seeking gay – Kapisa. Afghanistan.

9--I am really interested for a Handsome and nice boy for Sex - Kabul – Kabul My name is john and seeking boys. Seeking: I am really interested for a handsome and nice boy for sex. I am gay, 23 years I really love to watch TV specially sex programmes. Contact with johne: I am really interested for a Handsome and Nice boy for Sex – Kabul.

10--Sex - Phone - Khost - My name is Minh and seeking boys Seeking: sex - phone .I'm gay ... – Khost. My name is Minh and seeking boys. Seeking: sex - phone....

11--I am gay handsome Asian Afghan looking for friend for phone and fun, can meet contact with Minh: Sex - Phone – Khost

12--I need Sex with mature men – Afghanistan. My name is dariush and seeking gay. Seeking: sex with mature men.

13--I am gay, 31 years, I'm honest friendly and well experienced. Contact with dariush: Sex with mature men – Afghanistan.

14--I am also looking what u is looking for - Kabul – Kabul. My name is Najeeb and seeking gay. Seeking: I am also looking what u are looking for. I am gay, 25 years

15--Looking for friends and may be a long-term relationship if things go well. If you are just looking for sex then please don't add me...... Loverguyslove@yahoo.com and lets talk more. Contact with Najeeb: I am also looking what u are loooking for – Kabul

16--I like nice boy for friend ship, Sex – Balkh. My name is jan khan and seeking gay. Seeking: i like nice boy for friend ship, sex.

17--I am gay, 51 years. gay 50 bottom versatile. Contact with juma khan:i Like Nice boy for friend ship, Sex – Balkh

18--I Want boy from 14 till 16 years old - Kabul – Kabul. My name is haseeb and seeking boys. Seeking: i want boy from 14 till 16 years old.

19--I am gay I love boys I like sex my dream is that friendship with ramin jan contact with haseeb: I Want boy from 14 till 16 years old – Kabul.

20--Guys for Friendship and Sex – Kabul. My name is Najeeb and seeking gay

Seeking: Guys for friendship and sex.

21--I am gay, 25 years. I am very good looking...hahahha. My account is najeeb.ahmd@yahoo.com. Contact with Najeeb: Guys for Friendship and Sex – Kabul

22--sexes - Kandahar - My name is f and seeking boys Seeking: sexe .I'm gay salut moi ...My name is f and seeking boys Seeking: sexy. I am gay salut, moi h 45 5.10 215lbs musclé, bottom cherche top. Mon addressee repenh44 at live point ca, contact with f: sexe – Kandahar

23--I am looking for a man to Do Gay Sex with me - Herat – Herat. My name is shahin and seeking boys. Seeking: I am looking for a man to do gay sex with me.

24--I am gay. I am Shahin 30 years old i did sex with men in my child hood now I would like to do it again i have got accustomed to it i am living in Herat. Contact with shahin:I am looking for a man to Do Gay Sex with me – Herat. (Afghanistan boys for sex Afghanistan: MundoAnuncio.com / Todo el Mundo).

These are few example of sexual chatting in and outside of Afghanistan, but normally, Afghans are mostly active. In some parts of the country, most young and married people keep play boy.

The Treatment of Women in Afghanistan is harsh. They are treated like they are nothing more than a show piece. The overthrow of the Taliban in November 2001 raised hopes that women in Afghanistan would rapidly regain their human rights. Ongoing threats to women's security make their participation in public life almost impossible.

Afghan mothers further suffer given from the dismal odds their children face. One quarter of babies never reach their fifth birthday. In any given week, approximately 6,000 Afghan children may die, mostly from easily preventable and treatable causes like pneumonia, diarrhea, cool fever and birth complications. Poverty is the main cause of women plunge into prostitution industry.

The issue of play boy is more complicated in Afghanistan. Bacha bazi is illegal in Afghanistan, but the practice is still thriving. Boys are taken from their families at a young age and sold or given to wealthy and powerful business men, politicians, and military commanders.

By forcing them to perform in women's clothes and by raping them, this tradition not only seeks to humiliate these boys for the pleasure of wealthy men, but also to reinforce the idea that women are inferior and for a boy to have feminine affectations is degrading for him. The Taliban gone, the tradition of sodomy returns to Kandahar. Bearded men, accompanied by their "Aashna" (beloved boys) are again openly visible on the streets of Kabul, Kandahar and Mazar-e-Sharif.

The Taliban had forbidden the Afghan tradition of "play boy", the grooming of favourite boys for sexual pleasure. In one of his first acts in 1994, Mullah Omar freed a boy who was being fought over by two Mujahidin warlords in Kandahar, who had started firing artillery rounds at each other's positions, destroying part of the city.

A boy becomes a prostitute by being kidnapped by a militia, pressured to do so by a warlord or due to poverty. The adult clients are male, heterosexual and have more money and a higher social status then the boy or his family. As the men involved in male prostitution are attracted to women, the boys are seen as defacto women in a culture where sexual activity with a woman outside of a marriage is not only difficult.

Forced and early marriages entrap girls and deprive them of their basic rights. In forced marriages, one of the partners is not willing to participate and varying degrees of coercion are involved. In arranged marriages, the families play a leading role, but the individuals getting married can supposedly choose whether to marry or not. In many cases, the border between forced and arranged marriage is imperceptible.

The ordeal of Afghanistan's child brides illustrates an uncomfortable truth. What in most countries would be considered a criminal offense is in many parts of Afghanistan a cultural norm, one which the government has been either unable or unwilling to challenge effectively.

In the rural areas of Afghanistan, girls are mostly married between ages of 7 to 11. It is really rare that a girl reaches the age of 16 and is not married. The customs, traditions and community they live in make it impossible for girls to break free from forced marriages. They do not get ask to speak for self desire. The fathers in the families mostly decide, as the mothers do not get involved in the decisions, because they are women.

Despite recent efforts to toughen laws designed to protect women, the government does little to combat abuses. For example, the law on elimination of violence against women, which was regarded by rights activists as a major step forward when it came into effect in August last year, is not being enforced in many rural areas, where officials have not even heard of it, the report said.

In March 2009, the Afghan parliament passed a law enabling the country's Shiite minority to set its own family-law standards. The law was a serious set-back for women's rights--what modest rights women in Afghanistan have been gaining since the end of the Taliban regime in 2001.

The incidence of missing women is particularly severe in Afghanistan. The country has the world's highest percentage of missing women relative to its total female population. Census data from a study by Hudson show that more than 1.1 million Afghani women were missing in 2001. This is primarily the result of son preference, which leads to female sex-selective abortions, relative neglect of young girls (compared to boys) in early childhood, and the abandonment of young girls. Female genital mutilation, however, is not practised in Afghanistan.

Treatment of Women in Afghanistan is also bad because the women were not allowed to learn how to speak English so they might get a better job. They did not have cell phones. Treatment of Women in Afghanistan is horrible because they are not allowed to marry who they want.

Their husband is picked out for them. They cannot marry Western men. In order to leave the country they have to have a passport and visa. But unless they are travelling with a male, then they are not given these.

According to Pajhwok news report, women prisoners in the central jail, in the city of Mazar-e-Sharif have complained of the lack of health care, heating and food in the jails where they are held. The female inmates claim that the prison conditions are dire and they claim that they are sexually abused, but the prison authorities have denied these allegations categorically. The head of an Afghan children's rights group working within the Human Rights Commission told Pajhwok:

"We have not received any complaints about women being sexually abused, and we will immediately send a team led by Roya Dadras to investigate the claims." Mari, hugging her newly-born, one Month old baby says: "Our food is too bad. Four people have to share one blanket and we live in a damp room."

In 2010, violence against women attributed to or alleged to have been perpetrated directly or indirectly by the Taliban continued, the report said, affecting women at every level in society and from all ethnic and religious groups. The report highlighted the resurgence in the use of "night letters" to intimidate women who operate in public life.

"These 'night letters' are written threats delivered at night to a home or mosque, addressed to individuals... they are followed up with real violence, and in some cases murder," said the report, adding that the government's lack of action in identifying and prosecuting the killers of several prominent women undermined any confidence in its commitment to ensuring accountability for crimes carried out.

CHAPTER TWO

PROSTITUTION UNDER THE TALIBAN

What you are about to read by no means gives a panoramic picture of the suffering and misery of the most victimized, the most deprived and the most trampled section of the agonized people of Afghanistan -in particular of its ravished capital city, Kabul. The report which follows only serves to highlight the following points:

Contrary to the ludicrous assertions of Taliban and Jihadi criminals, the savageries of the "Islamic State" and of its substitute "Islamic Emirate" of Afghanistan have not only not had the slightest impact on reducing prostitution -this gross violation of women's rights- in the country, their "pious" criminality have increased the flesh trade by leaps and bounds.

Once again, in contradiction of the Taliban and Jihadi fundamentalist bands' ridiculously childish opinion, the scourge of AIDS knows no national or religious boundaries. HIV infection has long since infiltrated Afghan society and is rife especially among prostitutes where it claims unmarked and un-remarked silent victims.

The fundamentalist rulers of Afghanistan are too insensibly ignorant to appreciate the threat of AIDS. In their puerile, arrogant "erudition", they believe that by chanting their refrain-word "Islam", their Sharia will perform a miracle and fundamentalist-contaminated Afghanistan will be AIDS-free!

The "Islamic Emirate" with its perpetual pitching of the banner of "Islam" and "Sharia law" on each and every infamy, including stoning to death and arbitrary executions, can never hope to provide a cure for festering social ills, prostitution in particular. As we have asserted time and again, they can only worsen the situation.

One of the unforgivable crimes of each and every stooge regime -from Taraki to Najib-is the propagation of prostitution and the physical, mental, and moral devastation of Afghan women. Jihadi criminals elevated this disgrace to its acme. The more the Taliban hypocrites wrap themselves up in Islam and Sharia law, the more distinguished they become in shame and infamy.

The fundamentalists and their sympathizers put prostitutes forward as a defiled, untouchable group in their "pure Islamic" society and believe that the "purity" of their illusory "pure" society lies in persecution and annihilation of prostitutes.

It behoves our noble and patriotic intellectuals to point out in no uncertain terms that whatever ignominy that may be associated with the shameful flesh trade is a reflection of the mark of shame and disgrace branded onto the foreheads of fundamentalist rulers. These despicable rulers are most worthy of all contempt as they are the source and the cause of all social scourges, including prostitution, in our mortally wounded country.

Taliban arrival has increased the social and especially the economical problems of Afghan women. The women of Afghanistan live under monstrous oppression of both Jehadi and Taliban fundamentalists in disastrous situations where most of their basic human rights are denied of them. The Taliban denial of women to have a job has created a flood of unemployed women in Kabul.

These unemployed women face serious financial problems and as a natural consequence their children suffer from hunger, malnutrition, different illnesses and a chronic state of poverty. Most of them has have lost their last resorts of income and have sold most of their possession to buy food. Those who could afford leaving the country have done so, and those who could not are making the bulk of beggars in our country. A large number of these beggars are ex teachers and civil servants.

Bad state of economy especially in Kabul has hit hard the pity income of these beggars. The ban on female beggars to enter shops, inns and other trading premises is even further affected their income forcing a number of them to enter into prostitution for their survival, and survival of their children. A large number of young widows who are the sole breadwinner of their families and with all doors of opportunity closed on their face are joining prostitution as well.

According to a preliminary research on the problem there are hundreds of new prostitutes joining the ranks of professional ones. These women are mostly working from their houses termed as "Qalas". As the income from begging is declining for women the number of prostitutes is increasing.

Only in Kabul city there were 25 to 30 brothels actively working in 1999, which, for security reason, are constantly shifting residence every one or two months. Following is a brief report gathered forms some of these brothels in Taimany, Hashuqan-o-Harifan, Qala-e-Zaman Kan, and qul-e-abchakan areas of Kabul:

Each of these brothels had three to five women working and living in them. Some of the terms they use were; "Kharabati" for prostitute, "khala kharabati" for an old woman managing the work of the brothel, "Qala" for the brothel and "Qala dar" for their pimps. The environment is usually hostile and there are arguments and fights over clients. Each Qala has two to three Qala-dars and a khala-kharabati.

The male pimps mediate between the prostitutes and their customers. The old women are managing the internal affairs of the Qala; collect money from the clients, prepare food and do other chores around the Qala. Clients either come into the Qala or the women visit the client's house.

A third way is through a taxi. Because of its security risk this way is more difficult as the Taliban has banned the use of a taxi without a "muharam" (close male relative).

Therefore the prostitute takes a 6-9 year old boy with them if they want to work through a taxi. These children are usually witnessing the acts. It has been said that these children are being asked for sexual acts as well. A woman, M. H, told us, "one day I decided to work through a taxi, along Salang-wat Rd the taxi driver signalled two turban wearing men.

The two men got on the taxi and we went to Silo area. In their house they raped my eight-year-old son. I could not do anything. My destitute blackened the life of my son." Working through taxies is harder. Sometimes the women go without a client for days. Taxi drivers usually don't want to take the risk and get involved.

Women who are not members of a Qala are considered a security risk as they may report them to Taliban. The women who work in a Qala usually carry three types of identity cards. One id, showing them as a widower with children, is used to get aid from UN offices or Red Cross.

These Ids are not used a lot as they change place quickly and don't want to get involved with the local officials. Another id, showing them as a married woman, is used for renting houses and so on. If Taliban arrests them for Zena (crime of sex outside marriage) they use their third id showing them as single women. Being single helps they avoid being stoned to death.

As an example last year a women, (SH), resident of Gala-e-Mussa was arrested for Zena. She spent two and half month in Taliban's jail. Finally she paid six million Afghanis bribe to the judge of military court (Abdur Rahman Aqa) and were freed after receiving eighty strokes of lashes. She said, "Mula Abdur Rahman (the military judge) receives bribes not only from prostitutes but from pick pockets and gamblers. Sharia (Islamic Law) is applied only on those who can not pay."

60% of the money that the clients of these women pay goes to their pimps and the old women working for them. Fear of Taliban has reduced the number of clients. The average ages of these women are from 20 to 35 years. The hygiene of the working environment is quite bad. A large number of these women are infected with chancre, syphilis, skin irritations and possibly aids.

Aids might have been brought here by those traders who spend months in Arab countries and have visited brothels their. Due to present unfavourable conditions these women can not visit the doctors or use contraceptive pills. The traditional and old techniques put them in risk and often cause medical problems.

In addition to above problems the clients create headaches as well. (P) (Due to security reasons their names have been omitted) who is not more than 30 says, "What can I do? This is my fate. I was starving and that turned me into a prostitute. Men should have some compassion. Our clients are cruel. In exchange of 200,000 Afghanis they wants us to follow each and every whim them. They force us to smoke hashish, which has turned some of us into addicts.

Some clients expect us to do unnatural acts or other stuff.... Some clients leave with out paying, for not accepting their demands. Most of our clients are gamblers but there are good people among them too, like travellers or people who have problem at home.

Now a day's most of our clients are turban wearers. If we do not follow their whims (which are mostly to organize pederasty with young boys or unnatural sexual acts with women) they introduce themselves as Taliban and claim that they have come to discover brothels in the area.

Mrs F tells her story "a client, who introduced himself as Mula Salim Akhund (Taliban) said he was working in the local police station and asked for anal sex. He said he would pay as much as we wanted. The request was not accepted and he left the Qala.

On March 1999 I was arrested by few armed men outside my house and was taken to "Wulaiat" (police headquarter) and had to spend 20 days in Kabul's women jail. I was finally freed on lack of any substantial evidence. However I was given seven lashes before being freed."

Most of the complaints are against "turban wearers" who are Pashto speaking Taliban. This is because of their rough manners, not paying enough or threatening as they leave the "Qala" and sometimes they enjoy torturing the women working there.

The mediator for one of these houses in Hashuqan-o-Harifan, (MI) tells his story "Need and destitution forced me into this notorious work. My first wife is dead and my second wife and I have four children. I was working in a government office as messenger but after the Taliban I didn't get paid for six months and didn't have any other income.

My kids were hungry and ill. Finding no other way I interred into this job which is not with its dangers. A few days ago I was bashed by two clients and then robbed of my money as I was accompanying them back out of the area along a graveyard.

R, who is around sixty years old and whom the women around house call Ko-ko, is an experienced woman who manages the affairs of the house. She keeps contact with other houses and gets her money from each woman. She was a cleaner in a Kabul hospital before and in her youth she was a prostitute. She tells her story "during Najeeb's regime our Qala was discovered and I was put in jail. When they learned that I was a cleaner in one of the hospital they asked me to work as a spy for them which I accepted and they let me free.

I was spying for them for a while when the ward manager asked me to solicit sex from the nurses for him, for which I received good money. A couple of nurses fell into his trap. Those nurses were later recruited into KHAD's 11th branch; however a third nursed reported the whole thing to the head of the hospital that then fired me." She added, "All the women who had worked with me have their own stories. Each had been forced to this line of work; no one is satisfied with this work"

With Ko-ko's help we listened to the stories of some of the women in one of the Qalas in Hashuqan-o-Harifan. There are a number of Qalas in Hazrat St in Hashuqan-o-Harifan. In one of these houses four women by the names Sh, L, P and Z are working during different times. The house is manages by Ko-ko and a man (MI).

(SH), tells her story as follow "My name is (SH), and my father's name is M, S. I am originally from Kohistan in Parwan Province. Other women in this Qala call me P; G. my father worked in the Construction Company of Kabul.

"I lived with my two brothers, mother and an aunt in a very poor family. My father's wage wasn't enough and we were living by borrowing money from the people we knew. In 1977, I graduated from high school. One of my brothers left school unfinished and went to Iran.

My father was the only breadwinner of the family and he asked me to find a job. At that time it was hard for a woman to find a job. My father and I had to look for work and after a long time we managed to find a job in the ministry of public work."

The Minister at the time was Faeq who was from Saidkhail of Parwan and us being from the same region he employed me in one of the sections headed by Baqaie. Baqaie was from Panjshair, one day he asked me into his office and said, "if you do as I tell you I will give you a raise and a 56 kg regular coupon".

Because I got the job for economical reasons at the first place and I wasn't aware of his bad intentions I thought maybe the minister has ordered this out of kindness, being from his province and all.

However one day he said something to me which made me quite nervous and I left his office without mentioning anything to anyone. Another day when I went to his office two other women who were working there warned me about Baqaie's bad intention however before I could leave the office the minister entered the office and asked me to stay and thanked Baqaie for his services.

That day I got to eat with the minister and drunk something that I had not drunk before. Being affected by the presence of the minister and the drink, I was almost unconscious when Faeq (the minister) raped me. However that wasn't the last time it happened to me but repeated more than hundred times. I got pregnant. My mother learned about it and told my father.

My father beat me and wanted to kill me but my mother stopped him. She told him that he'll go to prison and then my father wanted to kill himself because he wasn't able to do anything to that minister.

The minister told me to stopped coming to his section for a while and paid me 1500 Afghanis. I went to a gynaecologist however the gynaecologist was saying that abortion is a sin. After I begged him he said he would do it if I paid him 5500 Afghanis and a ring that I was wearing. That doctor also raped me before the abortion. The abortion took a week to be completed.

My colleagues learned about everything and were offering their sympathy." While intensely crying she added "I asked for a loan from the ministry to pay the 5500 which owed but the request was denied. My salary wasn't enough for the house expenses.

I wasn't able to pay the rent, the electricity bill and so on. I was finally pushed into prostitution. One day when I was going to Sarai Hazar Gull a cloth seller by the name of Zahir stared at me. After a while we established a relation. I told him about everything. He promised me that he would pay all of my debts if I don't go with anyone else but him.

I kept my promise for a while but because I found myself totally lost I started going not only with him but also with two or three other men. Despite my income helping my family they intensely hated me.

I was growing stranger to my friends. The poverty of my family pushed me into this but I am also guilty. That dishonourable minister Faeq and his deputy Baqaie darkened not only my life but also the lives of tens of other women and young girls. In the meantime my mother fell ill and I needed more money.

I continued with my work and was making some money when the Saur Revolution happened. Faeq (the minister) was dismissed. I complained about him and reported him to Rafih and Watanjar but to no avail. Baqaie was promoted to head of "Asnad wa Irtebat". He was threatening me to withdraw my complaints.

While my mother was still ill I lost my father. During that time I was living with my other three family members. In 1985 or 1986, I was invited to join the Parcham Party. After a short time I was promoted and became the local secretary of bureau and also an official member of the party. Traditional morality was not the priority for Parchamies.

25

I was busy in recruiting other women and girls to the party and was even threatening them to join the party. Everybody knew about my past but no one could dare mention it now that I was a party member. I took part in house to house search of Cement Khana. I also worked in post offices. Others and I were slowly forgetting my past.

I made a little bit of money and was included in social gathering of the party. I might have pushed some innocent girls into the same ways that I was. It wasn't terribly important to me. I was accepted into the women organization headed by Dr. Anahita Ratibzad.

There were hundreds of women like me not much concerned over moral issues and quite easily accepting overnight rendezvous. Later I became a professional worker of the party in the national organization of women and was regularly sleeping with my "comrades" during night shifts.

Women's garrison and "self defence" were established under the umbrella of women organization. I volunteered in the garrison. Our place of work was "the Mairmono Toulana" where we were getting military training and I gained quite good skills in the use of arms. I was spending the nights with party "comrades".

There were more than 120 women in the garrison all of them professional workers of the party. I used my connections to send my brother to Russia. In 1988-89 I became a member of KHAD (Afghanistan section of KGB) under General Baqi. There were a number of other women and young girls. They were sharing in every area of the work not to mention the beds of other colleagues.

The areas that we were working were:

1- Administrative Section

2- Environmental and Art

3 - And brothels - there were a number of prostitutes in this section who were used for political reasons. Sometimes we were invited by Russian advisors in Microrayans area.

In KHAD in addition to security and espionage and house searches we were in the services of male members and a man by the name of Pasoon were managing our meetings with Russian advisors. I don't know how many other women and noble girls I pushed into the traps of KHAD and how many of them were raped.

I also participated in the interrogations of young and educated girls many of them were raped. It wasn't important to me as I was in it as well. In 1991 or 1992, I gave birth to a girl whose father I don't know. She is eight now. By then I was the head of my family. My mother did not interfere in my affairs but all other relatives and friends hated me and stayed away from me which continuous to this day.

When Najeeb's regime was destroyed and Jehadis came to power I stayed at home for a while. My mother died during that time. I returned to KHAD in Kabul and they accepted me and gave my job back to me. This time I was with Jihadist. The Jehadis were not less than Parchamites and were using the female workers for sex. Because "they were communists."

The Nizar council provided us with veils and sent us to Maidan Shahr, Paghman, and Char Asiab to gather information on the enemy. When Hizb-e-Islami (Islamic Party led by Gulbuddin Hekmatyar) entered Kabul I left my job again. With the money that I had I managed for a few months but when the Taliban entered Kabul I faced my economical difficulties again.

I left the house that I was renting, as all the neighbours knew about my past and I was facing more problem everyday. Finally I started on prostitution again. I knew some prostitutes when I was working in KHAD. I looked for them and found R (Ko-ko). It has been three years since I am working in this Qala. All the women working here have their stories. But all of them are working here because of their poverty."

I don't accompany clients outside the brothel anymore. A few times that I did accepted invitations to go went out, I was treated very badly. I don't take part in music and dance parties and only meet clients inside the brothel. I am very worried about my daughter's future. Although I am less than 30 year old I get very few clients.

The police and the Taliban do not pay at all when they visit us. The middlemen and Ko-ko get the bulk of the money, especially Ko-ko, she gets the lion share." (Sh) continued, "After the arrival of Taliban our business has been quite bad, our income has slumped and it is not covering our expenses. When Taliban learn of our whereabouts they ask for money and have sex without paying. We go without a single client for days, and live with lots of difficulties. All the doors are closed on us."

(L): Daughter of (GH. R), originally from Behsood of Ghazni Province is another prostitute who works in the same brothel in Hashuqan-o-Harifan area. She told her story as follow, "my father was an ordinary government worker. I was living with my two brothers and three sisters in a leased house in Karte Sakhi. I have studied up to year twelve and I am from Hazara ethnicity.

It has been two years that I am working with Ko-ko. The women around the brothel call me (Gh). My elder brother joined the military force during Najeeb's regime and later went to Russia. My younger brother worked as an apprentice for a mechanic. He was later conscripted and was killed in action. From childhood we were living in poverty, and day to day survival was a struggling.

My father never got a raise because of his Hazara background until he retired. My mother worked as a servant in Kabul's maternity hospital. I was a student at that time. Even up until the period of Najeeb's regime, despite our poverty, we were living a quite life and were thanking God for the piece of bread that we were receiving.

When the non-Muslim government of Rabbani and the Jehadi demons took power, the Hezb-e-Wahdat (Party of Unity, lackeys of Iran) established their military check posts around Karte-Se and started to control the Hazara localities of Kabul. The treacherous Wahdat Party was in conflict with other Jehadi organizations and because of that all Hazaras were restricted in their part of the city and we could not walk around the city freely.

The fighting between Wahdat party and other Jehadi organizations intensified and I was unable to attend school and also we had nothing to eat. The war destroyed most of the houses in our area, but our family was unable to move to another area. My brother was accused of being a communist and was regularly being threatened by the Wahdatites. One day some men from Wahdat party took my brother away.

Because my brother was a lieutenant in the previous regime the Wahdatites forced him to work for them in their military check posts and was later given the responsibilities of the check post in 'Khan-e-Ilm Wa Farhang' and 'Barikote' cinema. The Wahdatites were forcing each Hazara family to give a young man to fight for them or pay in cash. Wahdatites were saying that they had to hunt one Afghan (Pashtoon ethnic) and one Paghmani (a resident of Paghman, a district in Kabul) everyday.

The Wahdatites asked my brother to prepare a feast from them. I remember they had captured a person from Paghman that day. They took his bicycle and few hundred thousand Afghanis that he was carrying and then started beating him. I don't know what they did to him later. They divided the loot money and gave my brother his share. They put some money aside for the feast.

The feast was organized and a number of people with long hairs and beards came to our house. They were laughing on my brother because of our old carpets and furniture. They were calling my brother "Mr. Rezaie" and were encouraging him to loot someone from Paghman or surroundings.

They were reminding him that the people of Paghman have done so many wrongs to our people, and he should capture one and get some cash from him. "Killing them is not a sin" they were saying. My brother wasn't used to such acts but Wahdatites forced him to steal and to commit murder. Accused of being a communist and also he had worked in the army of Najeeb's regime; if my brother had resisted them they would definitely have killed him.

Hundreds of other men like my brother were killed for not following the orders of Wahdat Party. The feast was prepared in our house. I served the food and every one praised my hard work. However that feasts was the beginning of my nightmares. Among the guests was a man by the name of Qiadi. I noticed that he was staring at me in a lustful way.

I didn't pay much attention to it and didn't mention it to my brother. From that day Qiadi started to come to our house. Because he was a powerful man in Wahdat Party my brother was scared of him. He accused my brother of being a communist and was always threatening him my brother and was saying that my brother had to pay for his past sins. Despite the fact that my brother was armed and was working in a military post he had no real power and could not do anything about that man.

The fighting intensified even more. One day we received the message that my brother has been severely injured and we had to visit him along with Qiadi in the surgical hospital. My mother and I started crying and wanted to go to hospital together, but they stopped my mother from going to the hospital. I was very nervous and could not decide what to do.

My brother was everything to us. Anyway I left the house along with Qiadi. It was late in the afternoon and Qiadi asked me to go with him to the Party's health centre first so that he gets the necessary medical material as there was none in the hospital. I wasn't aware of the ominous trap that he was setting for me.

The truth was that my brother had been sent to another area on that day. We drove to a deserted house and he asked me to wait in one of the rooms for a few minutes. Without thinking I accepted it, I wasn't thinking about anything else but my brother.

Qiadi entered from another door and laughingly told me that I shouldn't worry, nothing has happened, my brother has gone for a mission to another area. He said that he wanted me to rest for a while and be his guest for the night. That is when I learnt of the filthy intentions of that treacherous Jehadi, but there was no way of escape for me. Like a small bird, I was in the claws of that bushy savage. I fought him very hard but to no avail.

Then I begged him to let me go I kissed his foot, I reminded him of my brother, my mother, and the food that he had eaten in our house, but it didn't work. Then I started struggling again. He asked his cook by the name of Qurban to help him. They together tied my hands.

Then he threw his cook out of the room with abuses. He told him that this is the way that the communists should be punished. I was struggling till very late in night but there was no one that could help me. The house was deserted with all the furniture being looted. Treacherous Qiadi finally got what he wanted and raped me.

Later I told him that I would be his wife and won't complain to anyone, at first he said no but then he swore on Quran that he would if I put myself at his will. He raped me a number of times that night. In the morning I told him that my mother might be dying from grief for her son, we should go and tell her and he should also ask her for my hand.

He agreed and said he would do it after breakfast. I was wrong. I was a prisoner in that room for another twenty nights or so. Treacherous Qiadi was meeting my brother every day and was pretending that he shares my family's grief. He was telling them that they received a false report of my brother's injury "I left your sister in some street and I went to the frontline". He blamed my disappearance on Sunni Muslims.

Qiadi had forced the owner of the house, that I was a prisoner in, out of the house. It situated behind the ministry of trade. All the furniture of the house had been looted. I was begging him every day and was asking for mercy. I reminded him of God but he did not even believe in God. Without a slight bit of humanity, he was doing whatever he wanted.

One day he brought two other men with him and asked me to serve them food without wearing any clothes. I told him that he had sworn on Quran and Ali that he would ask for my hand and would marry me. He ridiculed me and looked at his friends and told them that at the end he will give me to his cook, and then they laughed. That night all three of them were raping me till I don't know what time in the night. Qiadi freed me after two months and he moved to somewhere else.

My mother and brother had lost all their hopes for me when I entered our house. I told them everything. My mother was crying. My brother said that he would find Qiadi and will kill him like a dog. But I stopped him. I told him that my life has been destroyed, he shouldn't destroy his life. He did not have the power to fight that murderer and rapist.

We were still not able to move from that area. Also Wahdat Party had decreed that Hazaras should not move from their houses. A few days later Qiadi returned to our house with some armed men. My brother was not at home. He told my mother "where is that communist who has joined the ranks of Mujahedeen's? These communists are the reason that Mujahedeen's are going astray. They should be killed".

My mother wanted to say something about me but he kicked my mother and ordered his men to throw her in a car. My shouting didn't help at all. Around our house was all deserted. Because of our poverty and the cruelty of Wahdatites we were the only ones left there. This time Qiadi took me to Barikot cinema's check post where some women and girls of Sunni Muslim background were imprisoned as well.

They were being treated very badly and were dying under the tortures of Wahdatites. I was forced to cook for them during the days and was being raped repeatedly during the nights. This continued for ten to twelve days. Other women imprisoned in other rooms of the cinema were treated even worse than I was.

Wahdatites didn't care I was one of their Hazaras, they were committing their acts on whoever they could lay their hands. I was working during the days and was raped during the nights. They were saying that I had the taste of a communist, "These communists are something else."

They were saying. Repeated rapes and sometimes group rapes had wrecked my physical and mental health. I witnessed, with my own eyes, how other women were being raped. They brought people's wives and sisters on different pretexts and were raping them. I was missing my mother and brother and I did not know where they were. There was no way of escape and even if I had escaped I could have get caught by even more savage wolves.

I got pregnant but they were still raping me every night. My brother learnt of my whereabouts but he couldn't do anything. I learnt that he later left for Iran. My mother is gone with one of her relatives but I don't know where.

When they let me go I started working in other Hazaras' houses. My stomach was getting bigger. The husband and wife of the house I was living in got suspicious. I told them everything but they throw me out of the house. I aborted the child with lots of difficulties and got sick. A person by the name of Sakhi Dad Karbalaie, who knew my family, let me stay in his house for a while.

They started to treat me badly and I left the house. The disgrace that I had received from the hands of Wahdat Party had taken everything and everyone from me. Our destitute caused us to stay in our neighbourhood and could not move from there, which resulted in my brother working for Wahdatites.

At the end I was left with choices. I could sell myself or commit suicide, and that is how I became a prostitute in this Qala (brothel). I have no where to go all the doors are closed on m. My life is the result of the wrongs that the foul Jihadist has done to me. They turned my and my family's lives into an agony."

About her work she said, "I am still young, not more than 27. I don't have any saving from my income. At least I am not supporting a family like most others around here. I don't know about my future. Because of my ethnicity I don't get many clients as Hazaras don't work in the same brothel with Pashtoons and Tajiks."

"When I was thrown out of that house I was wondering in the streets for a while. I met auntie (Ko-ko). She is so experience that she had worked out that I had no place to go. She offered me to stay with her for the night. She said that she would protect me like her daughter. When we entered her house she congratulated other for their new colleague, then I knew where I had come. From that day I am working here.

(P) Was born in Kabul. She has been working as a prostitute for the past three years. She is less than 30 years old. She told her story as follows. "I left school when I was in year eight. My father was running a teashop and my mother was a housewife.

My father's income did not suffice our expenses; especially the rent and therefore we were always in debt. At the time we were living in Deh Afghanon. The young wife of the owner of the house who was living in the same house with us used to leave the house every day for some unknown reason.

After a while she became closer to me and my family and we became good friends. She used to come and talk to my mother most of the nights. My father used to sleep in his shop. During one Eid (Muslim equivalent of Christmas) she bought me a dress and asked me to work with her. She had convinced my mother that I should go with her to the city.

That day we walked around the city and she bought me some women stuff and bought a Pakistani veil for my mother. In 1988 my father was imprisoned for helping the Mujahedeen. My brothers were young and we didn't have any other income. We had to sell our teashop to pay for food and rent. After a while we were no longer able to pay our rent. The wife of the owner of the house let us stay in the house for free and convinced my mother that I should work with her.

One day she took me to an old house where a number of women and young girls were there. She introduced me to them and told them that I was their new colleague and I had to be trained properly. They gave me a pseudo name. I didn't know what was going on, and could not dare to ask.

The head of the group was a woman by the name of P. N, who was in relationships with many men and also had many contacts in the police stations and criminal units and was paying tax to them. Soon I learned that I had joined a female pickpocket ring. All of the women were professional skilful pickpockets. R used to take me to the city and train me in picking pockets.

(P. N.) Was managing the ring and was setting location of the city for each woman to work at. She stayed at the house and divides the money that everyone had gained equally after taking the expenses and her lion share and police tax etc.

I learned the skills quickly and used to accompany her in public buses. I remember once she stole 2000 Afghanis from a man very skilfully and gave 200 Afghanis to me as a gift. I slowly got used to stealing and became an expert. My mother knew about what I was doing but she told me that we don't have any other way. My father was in jail, my brothers were young, and how else we would have paid the rent and bought food?

I used to find victims in different ways. Some times I would have followed men from banks or shops if I saw that they were carrying money. I used to wear very tight and colourful clothes and attract the attention of men.

I would get close to them from behind or sideways and would keep them busy. I would show them some affection and men usually got comfortable quickly and I would cut their pockets. In the next stop I would said farewell to him and would have gone after the next victim. We preferred men's pocket. Women's purses were harder. I used to do this until 1992 1993.

I got caught three times but (P. N) paid bribes to people in criminal units and rescued me from jail. In exchange she increased her share. (P. N) was also running an illegal gambling house. (R) Used to go to these gambling houses and she took me along. After a while I became addicted to gambling. My mother tried to stop me gambling but I didn't listen. (P. N) help us got my father out of the prison using her contacts who knew General Boba jon.

My father when he got out of the prison he couldn't find a job. Because of my gambling I was in (P. N)'s debt and one day a man who introduced himself as a military officer and was from Uzbek ethnicity raped me in her house with (P. N)'s help. From that day on I was pushed to prostitution in addition to my gambling and picking pocket.

(R) and other women in the ring were prostituting as well. Because I was younger I was being paid very well. The crime of zena (sex outside marriage) was not that important during that time. I got a police record and officials of criminal unit especially major Habib Noor used to invite me to his office on his duty nights and ...

Rape of female prisoners by the prison officials was a daily occurrence at the Wulaiat (police headquarters). With (P. N) and Habib Noor's help I was freed from the prison after three months. I was meeting Major Habib Noor until he left Kabul. He had introduced me to tow of his police friends.

From then on I am alone. When I was in prison I met with every kind of criminals including prostitutes and middle-women. I wanted to leave (P. N)'s gang and met some women who were organizing work for prostitutes. I had their addresses from the prison. I started working for one of them as well as on picking pockets again.

I had a good income which could pay for my gambling addiction. I needed a lot of money and therefore I was picking pockets during the day and sell myself during the night. I didn't have a house or a family. I was going with anyone who asked. Nothing was important for me. I had lost my mother, father and brothers and I was missing them.

When Jihadist came I was meeting them as well. They were spending a lot of money and were good gamblers. But they were asking me to dance for them which I wasn't very good at. But they were offering good money.

I lost my pick pocket job when the Taliban came. They segregated public buses into male and female only one. Women were not carrying much money in their purses. I had to move to Ghazni Province. But there I couldn't find work too. I returned to Kabul and quit picking pockets. I was afraid of them cutting my hand if I get caught. Except for picking pockets, steeling and prostitution I didn't have any other skill.

I didn't have a place to stay. Nobody wanted my in their house. I had to go back to prostitution. I came to Ko-ko's brothel as I knew her for a while. I have been working here for a long time now. Ko-ko is making a lot of money on me. Because I am young and never had children he is charging a lot of money for me but keeps a large portion of that for herself.

Our lives are terrible, the brothel is unhygienic, the rooms are dump, and all the women in the brothel have genital infections and are infected with physical and mental illnesses. We are all going toward destruction. Taliban arrival has destroyed our work. We don't get many customers. The Taliban who come here don't pay and on top of that they threaten us to be silent. They ask for anal sex from women.

Finally she addressed me "Brother, if you are an important person, tell the Taliban to save us from the difficulties of high prices and scarcity. Don't beat the people but work for them. If there were jobs for everyone why thy steal would and lose their limbs. Why are we in these problems?

We ourselves hate our job. If I don't find a husband at least I will work for the sick in one of these hospitals and earn an honest living. Otherwise we have no other way. You people brought us to this day.

You people raped hundreds of innocent girls like (L) and destroyed their lives. Your are the actual sinners, you are the ones who used vulnerable not us. On the judgment day you will be asked not us."

(Z), another prostitute told her story us follows "my life was made miserable because of my jealousy toward my husband's friends and love for luxury. I have studied till class six. My husband became a military officer during Najeeb's regime.

 I was living with my husband in Dai-Burri. One of my husband's relative who was an educated women and was also a party member received a Macrorayan apartment from the Babrak's regime. She was showing off the apartment to us on whatever chance she got.

I got jealous and was burning to have my own Macrorayan apartment. I asked my husband to get an apartment but he told me to stop competing with his relatives and refused to do anything about it. Few days later without talking with my husband I got out of the house and started preparing an application to Kabul municipality.

I did not have enough literacy and also did not know how the system worked, which made me go around for months. I got disappointed for a while and stopped for a couple of years but then took up the case again and went to the municipality. In the municipality I met a guy named Karim.

He prepared an application for me as a homeless and he completed the administrative process for the application and gave it to me to go through the usual red tape of going through regional offices, party organisational offices and trade union offices. I completed all the process in a hurry, the papers were completed and were entered into a dossiers and became part of the waiting list.

I used to go and check the waiting list every now and then and got to know Karim better. My husband was unaware of the whole thing. After a while Karim said that my application has been rejected but I could have a chance in the second round. That rejection affected me very badly.

I decided that I should get an apartment in Macrorayan in anyway possible. After looking around for a while I met a person named Azizi who told me that he could get an apartment for me. I was wondering in offices for a few days with him and he lied to me that soon the distribution of apartments will start and a three bedroom apartment is under my name, but before we get the apartment he suggested that we have to celebrate the occasion. Finally I fell in his trap and let my self to his well.

After getting what he wanted he contacted another man who promised the key of the apartment and also we entered into a sexual relationship. But there was no news of the apartment. As I was losing the control of my life I decided to get the apartment in anyway possible. I told the two men to meet Karim in the distribution office; they accepted it and invited him. I met him for a few nights.

The nights that I was spending in Karim's house I was making excuses to my husband but in the last days he learned about my secret. After a year of fights and arguments we got separated and my husband throws me out of the house and told everything to my father's family. I lost my reputation and my friends left me. That was the start of my miseries.

No one wanted me in their house, and I didn't get the apartment. I didn't have a job or money and no one wanted to help me. I started to live in people's houses but was thrown out when men started to come in go into my house. My two daughters were with my husband. I went to the court but the judge said I am not a good woman and gave my daughters to my husband.

I was formally divorced. In 1988 and 1989 I was wondering the streets and found clients from buses and streets. I was in a bad financial situation. I got a job in the ministry for trades by one of my clients. My salary was not enough and had to work as a prostitute as well. After two years of work I was fired for having bad morality.

For a while I was unemployed and was going to clients houses. During that time I was recruited into 7th division of KHAD by a women named (S). in addition to spying and entrapment of men and women I was used for sexual purposes by the bosses on duty nights. My income was good. I was renting an house in Yaka Toot and had that job until 1991.

When Jihadist came I left my job and wanted to get married. No one wanted to marry me. I proposed to one of my colleagues in KHAD. He refused at first but then asked me to sleep with him and he will tell me later. That is how he said no. I was working in some of the brothels that I knew but my income was very bad. Fate brought me to this Auntie Ko-ko.

She took me into one of the houses and like a snake circled all around me. She told me that no other man except for the mediators would merry me because of my work and my past and has made me to work under her eyes. My unreasonable desires and wants and jealousy with friends pushed me into this job. I ended up as a professional prostitute.

Prostitution in Qala-e-Zamaan Khan:

In one of the brothels in Qala-e-Zamaan Khan region, two young women by names of (L) and (Q) are working. (Q) were away looking for clients or/and was begging and (L) told her story as follows. "she was a virtuous widow that was dragged to prostitution by bad luck, poverty and Jihadist civil war.

She lost her husband and was alone with two children and because she had no one, poverty and begging turned her into a prostitute. She has no one to help her. Her husband died after a few months of being ill, despite the medical treatment that they were doing by selling their furniture.

(Q) was alone. She was living with lots of difficulties. In Kabul no one helps you. Either you die of hunger or live as we do. The civil war among the Jihadist was raging in Kabul. Dostum's soldiers had their posts around Jada and Chaman areas. (Q) Used to go their to gather the leftover food from the soldiers." (L) who had heard (Q)'s story many times quoted it to us "I used to wear an old veil and looked for food in the military posts.

They were used to me coming and going and left some rice and bread which was enough for my kids. I was hiding under my veil and they didn't know that I was young. They used to call me "mother" and they told me "come here every day, we will leave you some food". One afternoon I went to one of the military posts at the end of Jaada, my veil were not covering my face.

Two of Dostums militia told me to go to the back of the building where they had left me some rice and cooking oil. I got happy and walked to the back of the building. I opened one of the rooms, nothing was in there. Suddenly, both of them attacked me from behind and raped me. To keep my honour I left the area without making a sound. I didn't leave the house for a few day.

Because my children were hungry I send them to beg for food. They were very young and no one was giving them anything. I was forced to go out and beg again. Begging wasn't enough. Hunger is a very bad thing. I couldn't put up with it my two children were asking for food.

I saw no other way. Poverty turned me into a prostitute. Those Jihadist who raped me were another reason to push me into this filthy job. Now whenever I get a chance I sell myself to men. Secretly from my two children."

(L) added about (Q): "Now she is working with me in this brothel. Whenever we don't get any customers she goes out and beg for money or find customers through taxies. She goes during the nights. Her tow children are getting older and she tries very hard to hide it from them. She knows a taxi driver who always takes her with him."

(L) told her won story as follows "My husband (D. M.) Was a builder. We had three children. Our life, although in poverty, was passing without any major headache. From our bad luck my husband fell from a roof while working and got paralyzed.

Treatment could not fix him. My husband lived for a while, during that time my brother who is fixing radios was supporting us. When he got married he stopped supporting us. My daughters had to stop going to school and our life got miserable. We didn't have food. I applied for a job in ministry of electricity and waters. They gave me a job as a servant.

After a while all of the workers including me were asked to attend the office of Parcham party's administrator for the ministry. We were asked to join the party, otherwise they said, we assume you are supporting the enemy. Fearing losing my job I joined the women's organization of the party. They gave me the responsibility of preparing reports on individuals who were working with me and to find out whether or not they are against the government and ....

I moved from my house to a suburb closer to the city (from Qala-Cha to Bibi-Mahro, party membership was dangerous in the outer regions of Kabul) and was attending the party meetings once a week. Nahid, a corrupt woman who was also the administrator of our women's organization would seduce good-looking young girls and introduced them to the ministry officials. I wasn't aware of this fact which made hundreds of women to lose the honour of their family. And one day it was my turn.

The administrator of the ministry's organization whose name I have forgotten asked me to come to his office one afternoon. He asked me something about the work and gives me some money as gift and then told me that I can come to his office whenever I had any problem because this organization was that of hard working proletariats. Next time I went to his office he was different, with very kindness he put his hand on me and finally he asked me for sex.

I told him that I am not that kind of women and "nobody had dared asking for such things from me before and you are saying that it is workers' party and you are defending their rights, now you are using us the proletariat" He replied that "this is not immoral, I am not forcing you or oppressing you. We will both enjoy it. Look, this kind of acts should be Ok between comrades. Comrade Nahid has no problem with it."

That day I went home without doing anything. Now that I knew of his intentions I knew that I was in a very bad situation. On one hand I was facing poverty and on the other my honour was at stake. My husband was not able to walk and I had to feed my son and three daughters. We had no supporter. My brother sold our house and without giving us our share migrated overseas.

Our problems were increasing everyday. My salary wasn't enough to pay the rent and buy food. I had the salary of a level-10 contracted-worker. The administrator asked me to his office few days later while being intoxicated and told me that I should work overtime as he knew about my problems.

And told me that he was doing it as a favour for me. I accepted the offer. The administrator was asking me to his office every now and then and was repeating his requests and that it was not unethical. He told me that I should concentrate on solving my financial problems, and I should do what he is saying. Sometime he threatened me and sometimes he was kind.

At the end he asked for help from notorious Nahid. She had said that "these women are still asleep. They should be wakening up. These things still matters to them." And one day she told me "Dear (L) your husband is sick and you have needs like everyone else, it is not such a big deal" and left the office.

Finally the administrator got what he wanted, and forced himself on me in his office. This act was repeated a number of times and I was in his disposal whenever he wanted. My husband died after a while, my daughters were getting older and I was working as a servant and a toy for the administrator. I found someone who wanted to marry me but when he found out about the administrator, he left.

Another person came and got married to my elder daughter. After a while she told him everything about my illegitimate affairs and my son-in-law threw me out of the house and kept my other daughter with him. My son went to his uncle and became an apprentice in his radio workshop. Although I am happy that my daughters didn't became like me but I regret not being allowed in their house. I did what I did because of them and now they call me a prostitute.

I left my job when people learned of my relation with the administrator. I was wondering around for a while and went everywhere that I got invited without any hesitation and finally I got here.

I am getting older, clients don't show any fondness for me anymore and I go without a client for days. Sometime I don't even get a piece of bread. My steady clients most of whom are gamblers don't come to me anymore. Only one or two of them still come but only when they have won money Because of security problems we have to change our house very quickly."

Prostitution in Qela-e-Aabchakaan

Three women and one girl are working in this brothel; they are constantly under threat of being arrested. The women introduced themselves as (QR), (F) and (N). The brothel is managed by a man, who did not tell us his name, and middle aged women (N. Z.). N. Z. told her story as follow "I am one of the original people of Kharaabaat. I have been doing this work for years.

I used to sing and dance at the weddings when I was young. I also worked as an artist in the Old Marastoon Sahna, which located in the Kabul mandawi. My youth passed nicely. My daughters got married and went to their husbands' houses; I don't have any son. My husband was an instrument player. When he died, a number of years ago, I lived alone for awhile.

When the Taliban and the Mulas forbade music and dance I started doing this work. I have been doing this for the past two years. We can not live in one area for a long time. When people learn of our secret, we move. Jehadies were good, they paid well, and especially the Dostumies were very generous."

Q. R. told her story as follow "We came to Kabul a long time ago. My husband (G) had a gambling house in Bagh-e-Qazi and also worked as a bus driver in Kabul-Qandahar highway. He was a gambler and gambled away whatever he could get his hands on and worst of all he was a pederast. He still gambles and commits pederasty.

When he loses his money he comes after me and forces me to give my money to him. During Karmal's regime he was imprisoned because of a fight in his gambling house, and although I didn't liked him anymore I tried to help him. I went to the head of Shotor Khana Police Station who was a party member as well, he told me that in addition to the gambling offence, my husband had stabbed someone and he told me to come to his office the next day.

The next day during talking to me he told that "you are a beautiful women, why are you married to a gambling addict. You should free yourself from him. If you wanted I can help you and we could get married." I told him that although he is a bad man but he is my husband and we have a child and we have lived together for a while now. He told me that he would pay for my expenses if I become his mistress but I can't go with other people.

I rejected his request and tried to free my husband from some other way. Because the key to my husband's freedom was with that officer my endeavours didn't get anywhere. One day that officer sent for me that I should meet him because they are sending my husband to Wulaiat (headquarters) that day. I visited my husband and told him about the situation. He said that I should do whatever that officer wanted me to do. I put my self in that officer's disposal.

My husband was freed and he moved to work in Herat Highway. The officer started to come to my house when my husband was away and he was paying for some of our expenses. My husband learned about the situation but didn't get upset he only told me that I should watch it because I am getting out of control.

My husband went back to gambling and left his job. One day he got into a fight and was imprisoned in Qandahar. I was meeting that officer regularly until one day he went somewhere and I didn't see him after that. I got broke and establish relationship with two other men. My husband got out of the jail after six months and came home.

He learned about my relations but didn't say anything. A week later he told us that we are going to Iran. I thought we are going there because he is concerned about his bad name and want to get away from it all. When we got in Iran I was thinking that he would get a job but alas, he was a very dishonourable.

In Iran we rented a house; he was bringing Iranian clients for me in the house. He told me that he could not work as labourer. I was selling myself for two years in Iran. When Najeeb got in power we returned to Kabul and bought a house in Shar-e-Kohna with the money that I had made prostituting. G started gambling again and lost all of my money.

In addition to gambling he had become a pimp as well, he had found other women and was bringing client to her house. My daughter was getting older and knew about the work that her father and I were doing. I am very careful that G may throw our daughter into this miserable life. Before the Taliban, this job did not have much danger in it but now we live in constant fear and we don't find many clients either.

I don't have a friendly relation with N.Z and the other man that look after this brothel. They always threatening me that if G doesn't reform his behaviours I have to leave the brothel. Sometimes G brings clients to this brothel, or he organizes for pederasty with some people from ministry of intelligence that he knows (one goes by the name of Gul Mohammad) against the will of N. Z. and my other colleagues. He brings beggar boys for sexual acts.

Last winter they had a fight over pederasty and our secret was nearly disclosed. We have decided to move from this house. Another reason for moving from this house is that some of the people that are coming here are asking for anal sex which is a bad thing."

(F) told her story as follow "My husband worked as a driver. The Jehadies killed him while he was working in Jabul Saraj and burned his truck. My children became orphans and we were no longer able to pay our rent or buy food. I had to borrow money and I am still under a lot of debt. No one is supporting us. I started to working in people's houses, washing clothes.

In one of the houses I got involved with a man. I received a bad name because of that. After that I became a prostitute and work as a prostitute for the past five years. Before Taliban I danced in the weddings to pay off my debts. I made some money and leased a house. I take my old clients or new ones that I find when I work as a beggar to that house so I could keep all of the money that they are paying.

Last winter one of the police from Deh Afghanan police station found out about my house and used to bring two guys with him one of them was an Arab by the name of Abdullah who used to pay but the other man wasn't. They have left the station and I no longer have to put up with them.

If I don't find any client I go for begging and if I don't find anything begging I prostitute myself. I have to find food someway. I live in constant fear. Taliban don't give us food and they don't let us beg, if they catch us prostituting we will be stoned to death. They never ask how we ended up here. If my husband was not killed why would I have become a prostitute or a beggar. Jehadi criminals put us in this situation.

N. Y. is the name of the girl who works in this brothel. She hasn't been married and told her life story as follows "my father wanted to marry me off to my cousin who I didn't like. I have studied up to year nine and can read and write. I was in love with a shopkeeper in Sarak-e-Qala-e-Mousa. Our house was around that area. One day I told that shopkeeper about my feelings but he apologized and said that he can not marry without the permission of his parents. I insisted but he did not accept and told me to get out of his shop.

When the Jehadies came I left the school. My mother went and met that shopkeeper, but he reassured my mother. My parents forced me to get engage with a young man, who was a labourer and I wasn't interested in him. Factional fighting had just started between the Nizaar Council and Wahdat Party around Char-Qala-e-Wazir-Abad and Nizaar Council established a post near our house.

My father started working for them as a cook which was a good financial help. Because of my father's job one of the men from Nizaar Council, who was a Parwaan resident too, by the name of Agha Bacha started coming to our house and we got close. One day we secretly went to the city where he bought a gold ring for me. My fiancé was a protective and hard working guy.

I continued my relationship with Agha Bach who was head of a group in Nizaar Council. One day he came to our house and found me alone there so he committed anal sex on me. He repeated that act a number of times until people learnt about it. When my fiancé learnt of it he fought with Agha Bach and wanted to kill him but he couldn't and he was arrested and imprisoned by Agha Bacha's friends on the pretext that he had contacts with Wahdatites.

Because of fear for my life and shame that I brought on my parents I went to Peshawar, Pakistan accompanying a boy that I knew. I spent a few nights in one of his relative's house but because we didn't have a place or money we came back. That boy didn't do anything to me but he said that sex with other people's wife was dishonourable.

He told me that I was shallow and untrustworthy otherwise he would have married me when we were in Peshawar. We got separated in Pul Mahmood Khan that is he left me and went away. For a while I was wondering in relatives' houses, those relative who did know of the situation didn't let me in their houses. To make a long story short I got here.

Because I was young and a virgin they happily accepted me in this brothel. At the beginning a good amount of money was paid for me to the brothel owner and they bought a watch and few dresses for me." She said, "I regret everything that I have done. When I remember my fiancé I want to commit suicide but N. Z. is watching me and doesn't give me much chance.

From the day that I have started this work all the men who come here prefer to come with me and because of too much contact with men I have contracted a painful disease which is hard to treat."

In addition to professional prostitutes who work in brothels a number of women, because of family problems, can not work in brothels. These women work on the streets as beggars and invite clients to their houses. It is an undeniable and unarguable fact that young women in Kabul because of economical problems, poverty and hunger join the ranks of beggars and ultimately go toward prostitution. These women number in thousands and their numbers are increasing.

RAWA Interview with some prostitutes-2002

Among the outcomes of more than two decades of war and destruction in Afghanistan, especially in the last decade when the reign of terror of Jehadi fundamentalists and their brother-in-creed Taliban were prevailing over the sky of our country, prostitution among our widows is a tragedy that can never be forgotten.

Unfortunately, as prostitution is illicit and secretive, there are no exact facts and figures to show the actual number of prostitutes. However, in keeping with the reports of RAWA members who are in touch with some of them, the number definitely exceeds thousands.

One of the projects of RAWA inside Afghanistan is to help the hundreds of thousands of miserable widows, some of whom have turned to prostitution and to rescue them from this filthy occupation. Fortunately, our members have succeeded in getting in touch with many of them and enrolling them in literacy and tailoring courses. Those women who are taking RAWA's tailoring courses are given one sewing machine free, so that by using it they can stand on their own feet and come back from prostitution to the normal and honourable life which is the desire of every woman.

It is worth mentioning that in the past few months RAWA has distributed food to a number of these women. In June 2002, two members of RAWA in Kabul interviewed around 60 women and recorded their conversation on video. Below we share a few translated parts of the videos. The pain and misery of most of these women are alike; the majority of them have lost their husbands at the hands of fundamentalists in the war and had no other way of life except to turn to prostitution. Their only desire is to find some sort of help and to return to a life worthy of human beings.

Your aid and support will give us the capability of rescuing even more of these helpless and oppressed women and saving the future of them and their children. Due to request of those women who have been interviewed, we have censored their pictures and have used abbreviations instead of their full names.

MH: She is a widow around 33 years old. She lost her husband four years ago in the war and has six children who are between 4 to 14 years of age. She was crying as she said:

"Because of my children I could not even commit suicide. For the last couple of months I have not paid rent on the house and every day the owner is threatening that he will evict us by force. I have not paid off the electricity bill yet, and make excuses every time the clerk comes for money.

During the regime of the Taliban, as there was no other way to make a living, I turned to prostitution. I was in contact with a Talib whose name was Sakhi Dad; he gave me ten lack (one lack=100,000) Afghanis per week. However, six months ago, Sakhi Dad left Kabul and I am in great trouble. My only hope is to find a job. I regret being a prostitute but it was the hunger of my children that pushed me to this. My older daughter is in the fourth class and I have tried hard to keep her ignorant of these facts".

FA: She is a 35-year old widow with five children. She lost her husband in the war between the Taliban and the Wahdat Party in Dara Soaf. Her eyes were full of pain and sorrow and with her eleven year old daughter by her side she said: "My husband was a farmer; while he was working in the field the Taliban attacked, killed people and destroyed the farms. They killed my husband in his field, and destroyed our houses. They killed my brother-in-law in the same spot.

We came to Kabul. There was no other way to feed my five children except prostitution. My eleven-year old daughter knows about my contacts. I have arranged an engagement for her with a boy about whom I don't know much, so that she would not face what I am going through now. My husband's family is poor and can't help. I am shattered and very worried about the fate of my children.

NH: She looks about 35 years old. She is from Paghman Province. She is the mother of six children; her older daughter is eleven years old. She is saying: "I studied in school till the eighth class, but when I got married my husband did not allow me to study further. Two years after we got married my husband became addicted to drugs. He beat me daily and made life bitter for me. He wanted me to work and earn money to feed the children.

When I was seven months pregnant he divorced me. I begged and washed clothes but that was not enough to fulfil our necessities. Nine months ago I turned to prostitution. I know that my life and my children's lives will be affected; if any one wants to help, I will leave this disgraced occupation without any hesitation.

FH: She says: "I am from Shamali. When the Taliban attacked our village, they destroyed everything. Everyone escaped to somewhere. The Taliban killed my father while he was working in the field. I moved to Kabul with my three children who are from three to seven years old. From that day my brother and husband are missing; perhaps they might be among the dead.

In Kabul I was working as a servant in one of the houses from where I started prostituting. Nowadays I am in touch with a jeweller who gives me money when I visit him. I am suffering from stomach pain and do not like to have sexual relations with too many people.

RA: She is the mother of three children, the oldest one five years old. When I asked her age, she smiled and said: "I have forgotten my name and you are asking about my age; perhaps 21". She is also from Shamali and has almost the same story as "FH".

"I lost touch with my husband in Shamali. We escaped to Kabul, but on the way there, the Taliban separated men from women. My husband belonged to Panjsher and my guess is he might have been killed there. I was two months pregnant when we left our ruined village.

I have been a prostitute for the last five months; there is a woman who guides me in this field. I have contact with a number of men who give me five to six lack Afghanis each week. My mother is a widow, too, but she doesn't know about what I am doing. I regret what I am doing but there is no other way out.

SH: I am from Panjsher valley but lived most of the time in Kabul. I had three children; two girls and one boy. I had a good life with my husband. But after seven years of togetherness my life took a new turn. Recently my two daughters died due to chickenpox. My husband blamed me for their deaths and used this as a pretext to leave me. He didn't take his son from me. I started this dirty business in the last few months.

I was living with my mother for some months but at last started begging. One day a shopkeeper made an offer and I accepted. Each week he gives me one and a half lack Afghanis. I don't know where he is from and whether he has a wife and children. I don't take any kind of pleasure in sexual relations with him, but it is forced on me. I used condoms to prevent getting pregnant, but in spite of that, I am four months pregnant now. My mother doesn't know any thing about my relationship with that man.

WH: I have been doing this for the last two years; I am widowed and must feed my children. I started with cooking and washing clothes but our condition was very bad. At last I got in touch with a woman who was a prostitute for a long time. She encouraged me to leave that hard job and do this business, which is full of money.

My first reaction was to refuse, but later on, when our condition worsened, I accepted. When I did it for the first time, I felt very bad and cried for many days. I am in contact with a number of men who give me money. I have been forced to do this and feel no joy while doing it. I am taking pills to keep myself from becoming pregnant. I always fear letting anyone, including my children and neighbours, know about my relations. If the neighbours find out they will throw me out of this area.

I am very afraid of getting AIDS or any other sexual disease; that is why I do this only in time of need. I am in touch with many women who are doing this dirty business and all of them are widows. I know Jamila who was killed by one of the Taliban's commanders. She had a relationship with the commander but when he found out that she had relations with other men, he killed her.

AH: My husband divorced me five years ago. I gave birth to two daughters but he wanted a son. With two daughters I faced a lot of problems. I started with washing clothes but at the end fell into this net. I have been doing this for more than two years. I am in contact with a man who has a showroom and he gives me money in return for sexual relations. He has a family, wife and children. I am using pills to avoid conception and I am a heart patient as well.

My older daughter is 14. In order to keep her safe from these things, I arranged her marriage. But because of bad luck, her life is bitterer than mine. Her husband is young and inexperienced and he and his mother do very cruel things to her. My daughter usually comes to share her pain with me. She is now a teacher in a RAWA literacy course.

FA: I have two daughters and two sons. I am illiterate. My father died some years back, my mother is alive. I was very young when I got married. We lived in happiness for some years but then my husband went to Pakistan and did not return. My life took a shocking turn after the loss of my husband. I have a brother-in-law who is jobless, poor and a weak man. I started doing it [prostitution] three years back when I found no other way out. I had nothing, no food, and no clothes for four small children.

I first started this with the shopkeepers. They gave me food for free. Sometimes they gave me three or four lack Afghanis as well. They took me into many places, in a hotel for some hours or a vacant home. I am using the coil to prevent conception. My brother-in-law is unaware of all this. But, if he comes to know about it, he will not care because he cannot help.

My brother usually comes home only at night for sleeping. He does not know anything about it either, because I am home at night. One of my children is weak and suffering from malnutrition. I took him to the hospital but it did not help.

AA: I am from Panjshir and living in the Saraji section of Kabul in a rented house. I am the mother of five children. I married one of my cousins who have been missing for the last two years. He was in Panjshir and worked with Taliban. Actually, Taliban captured him and did not kill him but rather forced him to work for them.

I had another husband before this who was a Mullah and died due to illness. I have three children from him and one from my younger husband. I lived with my young children in one home but they forced me to leave as they could not bear my expenses. When I left that house, they fought among themselves.

Finding no one to help me, I decided to go with this dirty business. Washing clothes and doing household chores for people was not enough. Whenever I go with someone, he gives me three or four lack Afghanis. I am still doing this twice or thrice a week.

SA: I am from Shakar Dara but have lived mostly in Kabul. My husband, who was from Saraei Khoja, lost his life three years ago when a rocket hit him and two of my children together. During the war we all had escaped the city to our village. We had a house there but Taliban burned that too.

After all these events (three years ago) I was left alone in this world with my two sons and one daughter, and I was forced to do this. My expenses were more then what I earned from clothes washing. I started begging at first. One day I went to a jeweller's shop to beg for money.

The jeweller said: "what a pity! Begging is not worth your doing." He asked me why I am begging, and I told him that you don't know the pain which is crossing my heart. He said he wanted to take me to his house for washing clothes. The next day when I reached his home, when I entered his house nobody else was there and he locked the room and raped me forcibly.

I could do nothing and he threatened me not to tell anybody and also gave me some money in return. I lost my honour, the only thing which I had left in my life.

Now, I am having contact with this man only. No one knows about this. His wife is a rich lady and often takes me to do household chores for her. I earn 8 to 10 lack Afghanis each month. God should not make any woman a widow. Nobody helps, neither kith nor kin.

I am using injection for contraception. I know the injection has its own side effects and that is why I am usually suffering from headaches. But, what should I do? Sometimes when I go to shops for begging, in order to pass the time shopkeepers will keep talking to me and give me a little more money. I am working for relatives as well, to feed my three orphan children.

GM: My husband is a driver and has been addicted to drugs for the last twenty years. I married 15 years ago. Actually one of my other cousins was supposed to marry my husband but she refused and my parents forced me to marry him. He is my cousin too. My husband, from the very first days of our marriage, mostly is out of the home.

When he is home I usually find him nervous and in bad health. I have often asked my brother-in-law about my husband's addiction. I had three children, one died due to chicken pox and the other two due to pneumonia. Now I have only one daughter who is 9 years old.

I started doing this in 1989. My husband was asking me for money every time he needed it for drugs. One day he sold off my daughter to a stranger. Fortunately I saw the man taking my daughter and running away, and I chased him. Another man who was passing by witnessed the scene and caught the man. I got my daughter back. After that day, my daughter is very scared of her own father; she does not even want to see him.

My husband says it does not matter to him how I earn money. In search of money sometimes even I go from Kabul to Panjshir. But I do take care to go to people who do not know me and are not relatives. My husband cannot live for a day without drugs and medicine. He is on his bed all the time like a small baby.

We are living with my sister-in-laws in the same house. Certainly, I do not want them to know about my relations and make different excuses when I leave the house. The men take me to strange places where I have never been before. I usually do this three or four times a week otherwise my husband will kick me out of his home.

HA: I am an orphan. My mother brought me up in a very good manner. I was able to go to school until class six in Kabul. My mother loved me very much. I had a happy and excellent life after my marriage. I am mother of two sons and one daughter. Then two years ago my husband got sick and died.

For one year I was able to earn my living in a very honourable way. But the situation becomes much tougher with the passage of time. Everyone forgot me. I was no longer able to feed my children. At last I began begging. A tailor by the name of Noor Ali (probably from Shamali valley) called me many times and promised to give me a good amount of money.

At first I turned down his offers, but then later I accepted to go to him for money. He promised to give me money weekly or monthly. I am still having contact with this man but my children are unaware of it. I have my father and mother-in-law alive but they do not help me. I would like to become literate, learn something, and earn money through honourable ways.

(RAWA report, August 1999: The RAWA was first initiated in Kabul in 1977 as an independent social and political organization of Afghan women fighting for human rights and social justice. The organization then moved parts of its work out of Afghanistan into Pakistan and established their main base there to work for Afghan women.

Much of RAWA's efforts in the 1990s involved holding seminars and press conferences and other fund-raising activities in Pakistan. RAWA created secret schools, orphanages, nursing courses, and handicraft centres for women and girls in Pakistan and Afghanistan. RAWA also secretly filmed women being beaten in the street in Afghanistan by the religious police and being executed. RAWA activities were forbidden by both the Taliban and the Northern Alliance. RAWA has so far won 16 awards and certificates from around the world for its work for human rights and democracy, some of the awards include The sixth Asian Human Rights Award - 2001, The French Republic's Liberty, Equality, Fraternity Human Rights Prize, 2000, Islamabad Emma Humphries Memorial Prize 2001,[14] Glamour Women of the Year 2001, 2001 SAIS-Novartis International Journalism Award from Johns Hopkins University, Certificate of Special Congressional Recognition from the U.S. Congress, 2004, Honorary Doctorate from University of Antwerp (Belgium) for outstanding non-academic achievements,[18]as well as many other awards. (Wikipedia, the free encyclopedia).

CHAPTER THREE

CHILD SEX AND MALE PROSTITUTION IN AFGHANISTAN

The story of two teenager girls who were forcefully married to wealthy and powerful Tajik war criminals in Northern Afghanistan, describes their torture, humiliation and imprisonment in the hands of Tajik warlords. Sajida and Rashida were barely 12-years-old at the time of their marriage. The story, though interesting, is ignominious. The recent sale of some Afghan teenager girls in separate incidents to Uzbek war criminals sparked concern about the protection of young girls in Northern Afghanistan.

Afghan Independent Human Rights Commission receives hundreds of complaints about the sale of teenager girls in Herat, Mazar-e-Sharif, Kundoz, Jaozjan, Shiberghan, Baghlan, Samangan and Takhar provinces every month. Recently, in Takhar province, a nine-year-old girl was sold for just $ 200 while in Baghlan, an 11-year-old girl was sold to a Tajik warlord for only $ 400.

In Paktika province, a young girl was sold for one million rupees to an illiterate man three months ago. These huge prices for a matrimonial life compelled thousands of Afghan citizens to involve in male prostitution. The Persian word, Bachabazi means play boy or 'boy for play'. As per its conservative nature, in Afghan society, women, either prostitute or professional performers, are not allowed to perform dance in the male parties. Therefore, in all parties arranged by warlords and their cronies, young boys are lured to dance all the night.

This is an established fact that a good-looking boy without beard normally becomes a status symbol for his master. Mohammad Zaher Zafari, head of the northern branch of the Afghan Independent Human Rights Commission, hopelessly said; "Sexual abuse and even the sale of boys has been going on for years. The boys involved are usually poor, underage or orphans and they are forced into it by their economic circumstances."

Another senior official, Hafizullah Khaliqyar, head of the prosecutor's office for Baghlan province, complained that teenage boys are forced to dance. "They are sexually abused, and they are even bought and sold. Fights take place over these bacha bereesh [boys without beard].

It is increasing day by day, and it's catastrophic," he said. A local Afghan reporter, Sayed Yaqub Ibrahimi, recently interviewed some warlords saying they play with dogs, boys and love teenage girls. "Some men enjoy playing with dogs, some with women. I enjoy playing with boys," warlord Allah Daad told Ibrahimi.

In the past, the Afghans used to be ashamed of it and tried to hide it, but nowadays nobody feel shame and they openly confess to indulging this shameless business. Religious scholars condemn the custom, which they count as one of the most sinful acts possible. Afghan ulema (Islamic scholars) are of the opinion that making boys dance and their sexual abuse is not allowed in Islam.

Maulana Ghulam Rabbani of Takhar province understands that those involved in it needs to be punished. Afghan police officers are deeply involved in male prostitution while the interior ministry in Kabul has recently received thousands of complaints from locals regarding the police sexual attacks on young boys. WikiLeaks recently released a cable from Afghanistan revealing US government contractor DynCorp's involvement in the boy play business.

DynCorp is a company of private militia training Afghan police force. According to recent reports, more than 95 percent budget of the militia comes from the US and part of that is being spent on child abuse parties and sex trafficking in northern Afghanistan.

To meet the sexual needs of Afghan police officers, in December 2010, as WikiLeaks cable reported, DynCorp purchased many young boys for Afghan policemen. The boys were later on used for sexual purposes. This shameless practice has also prompted the Defence Department of the US to hire a social scientist, Anna Maria, to investigate the problem.

DynCorp members and officers have already been alleged to engage in sex with 12 to 15 year old children and selling them to each other as slaves in Bosnia. After the WikiLeaks revelations about DynCorp's involvement in sex trade in northern Afghanistan, Afghan interior ministry carried out a thorough investigation against this private Militia Company.

The investigation resulted in the arrest of two Afghan police officials and nine other Afghans for the crime of "purchasing a service from a child". The US State Department began its own investigation whether DynCorp had ignored signs of drug abuse among employees in Afghanistan or not, but inspector general of the State Department in its report concluded that dancing boy incident is no criminal activity in Afghanistan.

Reuters, in its November 19, 2007 report and Revolutionary Association of Women in Afghanistan in its recent report quoted a 42-year-old landowner, Inayatullah, of Baghlan province saying, "Having a boy has become a custom for us. Whoever wants to show off should have a boy."

In his short interview with Reuter's reporter, Mr Inayatullah said, "I was married to a woman 20 years ago; she left me because of my boy. I was playing with my boy every night and was away from home, eventually my wife decided to leave me. I am happy with my decision, because I am used to sleeping and entertaining with my young boy," he told Reuters.

A recent State Department report assessed the situation, saying that it amounts to a "widespread, culturally sanctioned form of male rape". A majority of Afghans have no knowledge of their country's law about male prostitution. Bacha bazi and all other kinds of prostitution are illegal under the Afghan law. In Afghan society, the victims of rape and assault — both male and female — are sometimes persecuted rather than the criminals who abuse them.

According to estimates thousands of young boys have been subjected to this form of abuse, but the actual numbers of these vulnerable boys is not known. In Kabul, Kandahar, Mazar-e-Sharif, Kundoz, Takhar, Baghlan, Samangan, Pangsher and Herat bazaars bacha bazi CDs and DVDs are widely circulated serving an audience who cannot afford the real thing.

Bacha Bazi and Criminal Afghan Military Commanders

Warlords in Northern Afghanistan, according to press reports, recruit young boys for sex and dance, while local authorities remain powerless in stopping the practice. Bacha Bereesh (boy without beard) of ages 15 to 20 are normally dressed in women cloths, dancing all the night then abused by several men. The issue is very complicated. According to press reports, more than one hundred thousands Afghan men and women are suffering from HIV and Aids. Local warlords in Northern Afghanistan don't even know about the fatal consequences of prostitution and sex trafficking business. There is huge increase in the number of sex workers in the country.

US Department of State report (2007) has placed Afghanistan as a source, transit, for women, and children trafficked for the purposes of commercial sexual exploitation In Afghanistan, Chinese and Afghan women serve both Afghans and foreigners in guest houses and brothels. Under the Afghan law, sex trade and prostitution is often considered adultery, which is punishable by five to 15 years in prison. Tajik and Panjshiri mafia run hundreds of prostitution centres in Kabul.

The constitution of Afghanistan guarantees the equality of all Afghani citizens, whether male or female, before the law as well as the liberty and human dignity of any human being. The constitution also specifies that Afghanistan shall abide by the United Nations Charter, international treaties, and the Universal Declaration of Human Rights.

The new Afghan constitution, adopted on Jan. 5, 2004, provides for a permanent independent human rights commission, the Afghanistan Independent Human Rights Commission (AIHRC).

The AIHRC has reviewed the existing penal code and submitted recommendations to the judicial commission on provisions to combat trafficking. Any person whose fundamental human rights have been violated can file a complaint before the AIHRC. In this case, the commission can refer the case to the legal authorities and assist in defending the rights of the complainant.

The existence of 1.5 million drug-addicts in a country of barely 30 million is unacceptable. The country, already on the threshold of devastation as the legacy of three decades of civil war and highly dependent on foreign aid for financing even the most basic of its needs, does not have the resources to provide treatment and support to this growing pool of opiate-addicts.

Recent investigative reports have revealed some facts and figures about the play boy hobbies in Persian majority provinces. Persian transport mafia is deeply involved with the business and every two in ten Tajik truck drivers are involved in male prostitution. In Paktia, Paktika, Ghazni, Bannu, Waziristan, Zabul, Quetta, Kandahar and Khost, male prostitution is not considered an illegal custom. Every young and old man, if they want can have you boy.

Recently, I was told by one of my Afghan friends in London that some Afghan male prostitutes have claimed asylum in the UK due to their fear of persecution in returning to Afghanistan. They are sexually abused, and they are even bought and sold. Fights take place over these bacha bereesh. It's increasing day by day, and it's catastrophic.

To dress up their actions, the men involved in sex trade often insist these boys are to be dressed up in women's clothing and dancing in front of groups of paying men. Man-boy homosexuality has flourished anew in the aftermath of Taliban zero-tolerance laws, albeit a selectively punished offence in that era. Afghan boy are mostly turn to sex work and a life on the streets because they were fleeing something worse at home.

In the past, Brothels were openly allowed in the street of Kabul and they openly enjoyed this business. Islam doesn't allow such a practice and count it as one of the most sinful acts. Afghan Ulema are of the opinion that making boys dance and sexually abuse is not allowed in Islam. Afghan police officers are deeply involved in male prostitution while Interior Ministry in Kabul has recently received thousands complaints from locals regarding the police sexual attacks on young boys.

An intelligence website, Wikileaks recently released a cable from Afghanistan revealing U.S. government contractor DynCorp involvement in boy play business. DynCorp is a company of private militia training Afghan police force. According to recent reports, more than ninety five percent budget of the militia comes from the US and part of that is being spent on child abuse parties and sex trafficking in Northern Afghanistan.

To meet the sexual needs of the Afghan police officers, in December 2010, as Wiki Leak Cable reported DynCorp purchased young boys for Afghan policemen. The boys were to be used in Bacha bazi. DynCorp members and officers have already been engaged in sex with 12 to 15 year old children, and sold them to each other as slaves in Bosnia.

After the WikiLeak revelations about the DynCorp involvement in sex trade in Northern Afghanistan, Afghan Interior Ministry carried out a thorough investigation against the private militia company. The investigation resulted in the arrest of two Afghan police and nine other Afghans for the crime of "purchasing a service from a child."

The US State Department began its own investigation whether DynCorp had ignored signs of drug abuse among employees in Afghanistan or not, but Inspector General of the State Department in its report concluded that dancing boy incident is no criminal activity in Afghanistan.

This shameless practice has also prompted Defence Department of the United States to hire a social scientist, Anna Maria to investigate the problem, as several US soldiers on patrol often passed older men walking hand-in-hand with pretty young boys. There are thousands young boys undergone ordeals. But actual numbers of these vulnerable boys are not known.

Nushin Arbabzadah in her article (guardian.co.uk, 24 May 2011) highlighted some aspects of Afghan gays and their way of practice. "If you are gay and proud, Afghanistan is quite likely the last place on earth to show it publicly. How, then, are we supposed to make sense of the recent very conspicuous appearance of the rainbow-coloured gay pride symbols all over the streets of Kabul and other urban centres?" Afghan News Agency, Pajhwok recently investigated this phenomenon. According to Arbabzadah article:

Even more remarkably, Afghan drivers seemed to have little concern about using their cars to openly advertise being gay and proud of it. In a country where social conservatism sometimes results in gay men sharing their life with their partner of choice and an arranged wife so as to keep up appearances, there was certainly something very unusual about this apparently new openness. The rainbow stickers had first arrived on second-hand cars imported from Canada. Afghans had simply assumed that the colour combination was the latest fashion fad in the west, and duly adopted it.

The Rogue Afghan Army and Bacha Bazi

Some recent amazing news stories about the Afghan factional army collaboration with the Taliban, its active involvement in internal conflicts of neighbouring states and its killing of innocent British soldiers in Afghanistan have created misunderstanding between the Afghan and NATO military establishment. Soldiers and officers, associated with the army and jihadi groups, are working on different agendas. On the instructions of their respective jihadi masters, they kill foreign forces and play the role of purveyors for the Taliban militia.

An Afghan army soldier, Talib Hussein, killed three British soldiers he had worked and lived alongside. Talib Hussein killed Major James Bowman in his tent and then fired a rocket-propelled grenade into a command centre, killing Lieutenant Neal Turkington and Corporal Arjun Purja Pun. In November 2010, five British soldiers were killed by a rogue Afghan policeman they were training in Nad-e-Ali district.

On 17 July 2011, another British soldier was killed in Afghanistan. Lance Corporal Paul Watkins was fatally wounded during routine patrols with his troop. Moreover, on 5 August 2011, a fourteen years old Afghan teenager, Agha Wali killed a British soldier in Helmand when he was offered £50 compensation by the terrorists. Stephen Curley, 26, was killed in a roadside bomb. In another incident, on 5, 8, 2011, a British Royal Marine was killed in Helmand when his patrol was attacked by unknown terrorists.

These are few incidents that badly affected the credibility of the Afghan Army. According to a BBC report, Taliban infiltration into the Afghan army and police is a major concern as uniformed officers attacking foreign troops every day. As majority of Afghan Generals have fundamentalist jihadi background, they have recently adopted a non-cooperative policy towards neighbouring states and NATO as well. Their involvement in a massive corruption, land grabbing and drug trafficking transmogrified the military face of the country.

Infiltration of the security forces by the Taliban sympathisers is not new; on 30 July 2011, an Afghan.army officer was arrested on suspicion of working for the Taliban and plotting suicide attacks. Gul Mohammed had confessed that he was working with Taliban commanders.

Gul Mohammad is not alone in this profitable business; many officers of the Afghan intelligence and army are on Taliban payroll. To identify rogue elements within the Afghan army, U.S and NATO military command has begun to train counter-intelligence agents and to introduce an advanced biometrics program. Head of the NATO mission in Kabul, Lieutenant General William Caldwell, told reporters three months ago that some 222 agents had been trained for this purpose. Taliban say that the Afghan shooters in nearly every incident are sleeper agents in the army or police.

CHAPTER FOUR

CHILD ABUSE, RAP AND SEXUAL HUMILIATION

In last two chapter on Child abuse and play boy business in Afghanistan, I highlighted the issue scrupulously with a limited details, but anyhow, I received dozens of e-mails from Northern Afghanistan, Europe and Pakistan. Some Afghan vilified me for exposing the culture of male prostitution of the country but majority of my readers highly appreciated my shallow efforts. In fact, I have never been associated with any political or religious group in Afghanistan since 1964. I am a free tribal man of no political or sectarian background.

A background that elevated me to the skies is my intellectual and literary background which is my real asset. Last week, I came across a video on YouTube in which 12 years Old Persian speaking Tajik girl was crying of her injuries and bleeding in front of a local NGO. She was forcefully married to a criminal warlord who not only abused her; but severely tortured as well.

Her weak and beautiful hand was bleeding and torn cloths were blood stained after she got knife injuries in the hand of her husband. "Please help me get divorce, next time he will kill me, he injured me with a knife". She was crying again and again with demanding attention, but her crying and dismal face disappointed me and I got high blood pressure for two days.

Northern Afghanistan has recently embroiled in many hazardous diseases like HIV/AIDS, male and female prostitution. The main factors behind these diseases are considered to be poverty and unemployment. Poverty, unemployment, illiteracy and the culture of militarization produced innumerable smugglers, prostitutes, suicide bombers and professional criminals across the country.

In Northern provinces, poverty stricken children are sexually abused, while in Pashtun dominated provinces, children are being recruited for suicide terrorism. This has now become an unfortunate culture of the country. Warlords in both Northern and Southern Afghanistan arrange parties, invite dancing boy and pay them for sex.

As BBC reported the disturbing thing happens in the end of parties, is the boys are taken to hotels and sexually abused. This ignominious practice is against the principles of Islam and against child rights. Child abuse in the country remained a big problem while illiterate parents are using their children in forced labour to pay off family debts.

There are in ordinate cases of child abuse but only few are reported to the police. Parents don't want to report case of the abuse of their children to the police because they understand that police is already abusing innocent children in many ways. According to the article 54 of the constitution of Afghanistan; "Family is the fundamental unit of society and is protected by the state.

The state shall adopt necessary measures to ensure physical and psychological well being of family, especially of child and mother, upbringing of children and the elimination of traditions contrary to the provisions of sacred religion of Islam."

After the fall of the Taliban regime in 2001, in the penal code of 1976 law is still in practice with various provisions. Article 398 sets punishment for honour killings, adultery, fornication and homosexuality.

Article 427 describes long term prison for adultery and also increases the available punishment if a "violation of honour killing". Afghan Constitution is only on papers, both the police and government neither official nor ordinary Afghan know about their country constitution.

Regretfully, being an Islamic country, the business of drugs, children and women trafficking, Bacha Bazi and dancing clubs have undermined the so called Afghani Ghairat, Pashtunwali and love to Islam. Bacha baze is in no way acceptable in Islam while Islam is being misinterpreted in the country. Children have rights in Islam but they have no access to education, house, job, health and basic rights.

The streets of Afghan cities are full of working children, some polish shoes, some beg, some gather plastic bottles to resell and some are kidnapped for male prostitution. Last month, in Herat province, a 14 year old boy complained about his rape but didn't report to the police.

Afghan hospitals are full of raped and abused children who receive medical treatment for their physical injuries. Article 427 of Afghanistan's penal code determines "long term" imprisonment for adultery. The article further elucidates that child abuser can be jailed for six to 10 years. Normally, Bach Bazi or child sex in the country is within the context of sexual acts with boys, in which adult men buy sexual favours from young boys with money or gifts.

In this business, Private and pro-government militias have been found deeply involved. These Companies promote child recruitment and child abuse. Underage children are often abused sexually, tortured and put into hard labour.

Afghan government and US/NATO forces have set up community-based militias of bachabazi addicted men such as the Afghan Local Police, in troubled provinces who have free hand and they do every thing whatever they want. Children in Afghanistan are suffering disastrous level of abuse; they are abused and insulted both in society and within homes. Afghan prisons, they are tortured and raped. Torture and sexual assaults in Prisons presents a grim picture of scant respect for human rights.

The ways of torture of the Afghan police and security agencies are beating by stick, scorching bar, or iron bar; flogging by cable; battering by rod; electric shock; deprivation of sleep, water, and food; abusive language; sexual humiliation; and rape.

Another painful story revealed by Wiki Leaks recently describes the involvement of foreign contractors in child abuse, training of Afghan policemen who take drugs and pay for young boys. Afghanistan's sex industry is booming, according to both private and official sources. Statistics are scattered, and few solid figures exist.

To address the issue properly, News and Media Radio reported (2011) Afghan government signed a formal agreement with the UN to ban the recruitment of children into the armed forces and stop the sexual abuse of young boys by the military commanders and warlords. The culture of play boy, dancing boy or BachaBazi must be undermined, warned the UN.

Prominent Afghan journalist, Sayed Yaqub Ibrahimi has recently interviewed some Afghan prostitutes for their compulsions and way of business. For example a woman told Ibrahimi:

"I do not enjoy being with men. I hate them. But to keep them as loyal customers, I pretend," said the young Afghan woman. Dressed in jeans and a tee-shirt, with shoulder-length black hair and wearing no makeup, 21-year-old Saida (not her real name) looked ordinary enough. But in this highly conservative society, she has sex with men for money, sometimes several times a night. Saida's father and older brother were killed in the civil war of the Nineties and she lives with her mother and younger siblings in the northern city of Mazar-e-Sharif. She has been a prostitute for six years, since the day her mother made a deal with a local pimp. "One day an old woman came to our house," She talked to my mother, and then took me to a house. A man almost 30 years old was waiting for me. He attacked me right away. It was horrible. I knew nothing; I felt only pain."

Afghanistan's sex industry is booming, according to both private and official sources. Statistics are scattered, and few solid figures exist. But since the fall of the Taliban regime in late 2001, prostitution has become, if not more widespread, at least more open.

A police official in the northern province of Jowzjan, speaking on condition of anonymity, said that according to official figures, 2,000 families in his province alone had resorted to prostitution over the past 10 years. The true figure is likely much higher. "The main factor is the lack of employment opportunities," he said. In many cases, prostitution becomes a hereditary trade, passed on from mother to daughter.

The police say they are clamping down on prostitution. "We are quite serious about eliminating these centres of prostitution," said General Sardar Mohammad Sultani, the police chief in Balkh province, of which Mazar-e-Sharif is the main town. "Now no one dares to do this openly. If there are such centres, they are hidden, and those who use them are so skilled that the police do not know they are there."

An Afghan woman activist, Wazhma Frogh has he own investigative story about the women of Afghanistan. According Wazhma Frogh assessment of Afghan prostitution:

"In my work on women's issues in Afghanistan, I came across many women who have at least once sold their bodies to earn a living either forced by a family member or in secret. However, I chose to write about these three women I met three years ago in an old city of Kabul. These three different women have at least one thing in common, that even in a closed traditional and religious society; they were made to be prostitutes, either in public or in secret. A couple of years ago, I was on a monitoring visit to a rehabilitation centre for drug addicts and during the distribution of medical kits for the rehabilitated patients, noticed three women getting the medicine who didn't seem as patients. They were quiet well-dressed and the red lipstick was shining on the faces."

CHAPTER FIVE

AFGHAN CRIMINAL MILITIAS, CHILDREN, WOMEN AND DRUG TRAFFICKING IN AFGHANISTAN

The recent news stories about the women, men and children trafficking in Afghanistan have become a hot topic in world print and electronic media and intellectual forums. From Northern Afghanistan, recently, I received heartbreaking e-mails about the US military contractors' involvement in women, men and children trafficking in the country. These e-mails raise many questions regarding the NATO war on Afghan women and children.

Every month, hundred of Afghan children, women and unemployed young men are kidnapped, imprisoned or trafficked to international market and local prostitution industry in Northern Afghanistan. From Bosnia to Iraq and from Pakistan to Afghanistan, US private militias and defence contractors have left a shameful record of child sex, children trafficking, kidnapping and play boy business.

In Afghanistan, majority of orphan, poor and maroon children became the victim of these sex hungry beasts who not only sexually abuse them but share with friends as well.

According to the State of the World's Mothers 2011 report, published on 24 June by NGO Save the Children, about 50 women die in childbirth each day in Afghanistan. One in three is physically or sexually abused and the average life expectancy of women is 44. It said that more than 85 percent of Afghan women are illiterate, while 70 percent of school-age girls do not attend school for various reasons - conservative parents, lack of security, or fear for their lives.

Afghanistan's Independent Human Rights Commission recently voiced about the surge in women and child trafficking in the country. In its latest report, AIHRC has warned that: *"human traffickers used coordinated methods to allure women and children to take them outside the country. Poverty, unemployment, corruption and insecurity as the factors behind an increase in human trafficking. After women and children are trafficked out of the country, they get sexually abused and face other sorts of violence."*

On June 8, 2011, in Takhar province two small girls and a woman had been raped by armed men of a Tajik commander. Family members of the victims said government didn't arrest them. A six-year old girl was also among the victims. However, the district chief of Warsaj said five of the rapists had been arrested.

Ghulam Nabi Hakak, advisor and member of the supervision, assessment and reporting section of the AIHRC, told reporters that 17-year old Sahifa was detained by the police a few months back when she was trying to escape to Jalalabad due to domestic violence in her family.

According to the report of the AIHRC, Sahifa had been exchanged in marriage (badal) and she had fled from her home due to the cruelties of her husband's family towards her. Mr. Hakak said the Supervision of Women's Affairs of Kunar Province had placed Sahifa in the homes of one of the influential people instead of a shelter for her safety. He said, "After a while the girl claimed that she had been raped and sexually harassed."

Rapists in Afghanistan too often get away with their crime, whilst rape victims lack access to justice and experience stigma and shame, according to a report by the Office of the UN High Commissioner for Human Rights (OHCHR). The sons of a female member of the Provincial council of Helmand, who raped a child, were still free from the hold of the law despite repeated demands and the orders of the authorities.

Not everyone has the ability to watch the extremely shocking video clip of this rape, which has reached Kabul as well. In this clip Farid and Feroz, the sons of Bibi Laiqa who is a member of the Provincial Council of Helmand, rape the young son of Jalil Ahmad (also named Feroz) who was a resident of the Garshak District. The boy screamed; begged them to stop for the sake of the Quran but the rapists didn't listen to a word and continue raping him.

The child hided his face with his hands but the rapists threatens him to show his face so that it is caught in the video. There are other people with the rapists as well who were recording the video and one of the rapists said, "Feroz if you cry, I swear to God I will distribute it (the video) to the whole market."

According to the documents, a copy of which PAN got, Jalil Ahmad father of the child wrote the petition on October 3, 2009. In the petition it is clearly written that Feroz and Farid, sons of Mohammad Daud had raped his son; they had been detained but escaped. It has been demanded from the Governor (Gulab Mangal) that the father of the rapists is called so that his sons come and get punished.

The US State Department in its report on trafficking in persons for 2010 has revealed that trafficking of human being in Afghanistan is more prevalent than transnational trafficking, and the majority of victims are children. Poor and unemployed Afghan children are being trafficked within the country and sent to male prostitution centres. Forced begging is controlled by mafia groups within and outside the government circles. Begging the most profitable industry that finances insurgency, ethnicity and weapon industry.

In all 34 provinces of the country thousands men, women and children are begging on behalf of underground mafia groups. Organized and professional criminal gangs in big cities collect million in Afghan currency from across the country and share it with their friend within the government departments.

The begging women perform two jobs; prostitution and fund raising. Young girls visit the houses of dignitaries, parliamentarians, police officers, army generals and foreign contractors.

The US report warns that some Afghan families willingly sell their young children in prostitution, including Bacha Bazi and dancing clubs. The presence of Chinese, Iranian, Pakistani, Indian, Tajikistani, Uzbek, Turkmen, Uganda and Afghan prostitutes in various provinces of Afghanistan infected thousands illiterate people with HIV and AIDS. According to some unconfirmed reports, there is more than 50.000 thousands Afghan suffering from HIV infection.

The US human trafficking report has revealed that: *"brothels and prostitution rings are sometimes run by foreigners, sometimes with links to larger criminal networks. Tajik women are also believed to be trafficked through Afghanistan to other countries for prostitution. Trafficked Iranian women transit Afghanistan en route to Pakistan."*

Ten years ago, George W. Bush had warned that any US employee or soldier founded involve in sex trafficking must be punished but today there is no punishment and US private military companies earn a lot of money from the business. In Monthly Cutting Edge, Nick Schwellenbach and Carol D. Leonnig (July 26th 2010) have painted a painful story about the involvement of US contractors in sex trafficking in Bosnia, Afghanistan and Iran:

"Nearly a decade after Dyncorp International LLC employees were implicated in Bosnia for buying and selling women from throughout Eastern Europe — and not prosecuted — the U.S. Army was told this February that supervisors of an Army subcontractor in Iraq had sexually assaulted women who were held in involuntary servitude."

On the involvement of US contractors in child sex in Afghanistan, Joseph Farah's G2 Bulletin has reported a US military contractor's involvement in child sex (Bacha Bazi) who dressed up young boys in woman dress so as to present for dance in a party and potentially to be sold for sex.

The cultivation of over thirty millions mines in agricultural land across Afghanistan by the former Soviet Union and Afghan communist regimes transformed the country into a narco state. With this inhuman move, seventy percent agricultural land has became desert. It will take ten years more cleaning up the 30 million mines. Another problem that drags people into prostitution and child sex business is drug trafficking in Afghanistan.

Drug trafficking and cultivation not only promotes the Taliban insurgency but creates criminal trade and economic infrastructure. People and the Government in the country, are now mostly dependent on criminal trade and containerized market economy. During the last thirty years civil war and the absence of good governance, warlords and political leadership, with their gun power promoted drug trafficking, containerized market economy and violence.

Afghan drugs and China White Heroin are the main source of militarization and prevailing insurgent culture in both Pakistan and Afghanistan. Twenty million people in both the countries, specifically adults and women now using opium, heroin and other illicit drugs. Afghanistan is the global production centre of heroin.

There has been a significant rise in drug production since the US intervention in 2001. Drug trafficking in the country has mostly enriched religious and political leadership and the terrorist Taliban networks in FATA, Southern and Northern Afghanistan and Waziristan regions.

Officials of various departments in the country are deeply involved in this profitable business. Members of the Afghan National Army and Afghan National Police have become part of this business. The recent urine test of the Afghan police showed one thousand two hundred of them were found addicted to hard drugs, mostly heroin and opium. Not only had this, A Government Accountability Office Report for the United States Congress, in 2009 noted the some forty one percent of Afghan police using heroin, hashish and opium.

As mentioned earlier, high ranking officers of the Afghan police are associated with different narco networks and protect drug lords. For example, as Afghan newspapers reported the arrest of former Afghan police general Mulam Khan jailed for 10 years and fined $ 14,000 for helping drug traffickers in three provinces. Mulam Khan was the commander of Afghan border police controlling three provinces (Herat, Farah and Badghis provinces).

He was arrested in corruption charges over the smuggling of 660 Kg of opium. Afghan prosecutors accused Mulam Khan that he received $ 93,000 in bribes. The court sentenced him to ten years in prison.

This prevailing containerized criminal trade has harmed the military, social and economic infrastructure of Afghanistan, Pakistan and Russian as well. Russian Government has put anti-narcotics efforts in Afghanistan at top of international agenda

Russian sees Afghan drug economy as a grave problem, and wants to extend its anti narcotic efforts to the territory of Afghanistan. Russia is the world's largest consumer of Afghan heroin. Government figures point to staggering 30-40,000 deaths each year as a result of overdoses, with an estimated total of 2.5m users.

There are over one million people suffering from HIV positive across Russia. Russia is still a weak state in term of law enforcement. Here, a question arises that if the whole crops are destroyed across Afghanistan, not only the Taliban will lose revenues from opium taxation but farmers would be plunged in immediate distress.

Russian President Medvedev recently warned that international narco-aggression', is a greater threat to Russia than international terrorism. Any political games around this huge problem are unacceptable; they weaken our common anti-drugs coalition," Medvedev warned.

According to Russian authorities, Drug trade or trafficking in Afghanistan is worth $60 billion a year and its participants have no intention of giving it up voluntarily. Prime Minister Vladimir Putin has recently warned that the battle against drugs is not getting any easier. President Putin warned that international terror organizations, settled at the Pak-Afghan border areas receive financial assistance from drug trade and drug lords.

According to Russian sources, NATO and Russian authorities view the involvement of Pakistan and Afghanistan in fight against drug trafficking as a priority and at the end of 2010, Russia and NATO are going to invite Pakistan to join in the anti-drug project.

Moscow has recently proposed a joint fight against the cultivation and smuggling of narcotics in Afghanistan. Russian authorities say revenue from heroin trafficking is annual turnover:

"$18 billion but the distribution of royalties going to terrorist organizations are $15 billion, small wholesale traders $1 billion, narcotics labs in northern Afghanistan: $1 billion, Taliban: $30 billion and proceeds to peasants in southern Afghanistan: $100 million." This is a lot of money ($30 billion) going to the Taliban networks in both Pakistan and Afghanistan.

The global market for opiates is about $65 billion. European states consume 771 tonnes of these drugs. More than 100 countries suffer from this problem. Russian has recently repudiated NATO forces in Afghanistan for their failure in eradicating opium production and warned that drug trafficking was endangering Russia's national security. Public Security Minister of the Chinese Government has warned that due to the failure of the US-led Coalition in Afghanistan, Afghan drugs reached Chinese market as well.

This drug trade from 4.3 metric tons of heroin in 2009 and to six metric tons in the first five months of 2010. "The U.S. president's anti-drug strategy is aimed at preventing and treating drug use, but not at targeting opium production in Afghanistan, Russia's drug control chief complains." Experts in America say that the National Drug Control

Strategy announced by the US President recently, shifts the emphasis from fighting a war on drugs and poppy eradication to treating drug users.

The smuggling and cultivation of narcotics, according to Russian authorities, promote corruption in Afghanistan as thousands of Government officials are involved in this trade. Two months ago Afghan Ministers were accused of embezzling million dollars.

Afghan News Agency, Pajhwok reported the arrest of Hajj and Auqaf Ministry's cashier accusing Second Vice President of Afghanistan and seven other Ministers of embezzling one million dollars during last year's Haj ritual. Haji Mohammad Noor, who was arrested with $3, 62,000 at Kabul airport revealed that some Ministers were the real culprits behind the fraud.

These and other Afghan officials transferred million dollars abroad. Members of Taliban and high ranking officials of various Ministries in Afghanistan are jointly running the business of narcotics and drug addiction. They are close partners in this business. A UN report says more than 100,000 people are killed through the Afghan opium every year.

Experts say, in order to stabilize Afghanistan, the issue of drug trafficking is to be addressed, because this business provide financial support to criminal organizations that undermine stability.

President Hamid Karzai is under pressure inside the country to expel the corrupt officials from various institutions. According to American investigators Director of National Intelligence has complained that the US Government doesn't want to arrest some narco lords.

Afghan officials say, the destruction or eradication of poppy fields is not the solution; the solution is the agricultural reforms in Afghanistan, where roughly three quarters of the population are farmers. Majority of these farmers depends on the cultivation of narcotics. I think, undermining the poppy fields would deprive the larger part of the Afghans of a substantial portion of their income.

In 1989 when Russia withdrew its forces out of Afghanistan, the Mujahedeen's who were being supported militarily and financially by external forces had to face a decline in support.

As a result, the Mujahedeen's had to dig out their own means of generating economic and military support for themselves. But, as there were no other sources of generating income available in the country the dependence was further laid on poppy cultivation.

By 1992, Mujahedeen took over Kabul, but not with a very strong central command, thus resulting into fragmentation of the county into many tribes and groups. The individual warlords took no interest in strengthening the central government and each started living on his own. Again the only source that was available for their financial support was opium.

Thus, they did their best to provide the ever thirsty market with huge productions. By the mid 90's Afghanistan produced 2,200 to 2,400 metric tones of opium each year. The fragmentation of the country at the same time provided an opportunity to Taliban to seize power. In 1996, Taliban were able to gain control of most parts of the country and with a comparatively stronger central government in Kandahar.

The reign of Taliban further organized the narcotics industry, as they also had to generate resources for themselves after being left without proper support from their earlier supporters. Narcotics at that time became a part of organized crime in Afghanistan and better international connections were made available for its business.

In the first year of Taliban's reign, there was a considerable rise in the production. In 1997/98 total production was 2,700 metric tones, which was a 43% rise as compared to previous year. In 98/99 the production reached to its peak at 4,500 metric tones, representing three quarters of world supply. During the same era there was a draught in the country that reduced the food production to a very miserable extent.

With the developments in all the other areas of the country, it is really unfortunate that there has been development in the industry of narcotics as well. The processes of production and smuggling of narcotics have turned complex. Now, it would not be sufficient to say that land lords are individually involved in the processes and the economic crisis is responsible for its opium production.

CHAPTER SIX

WHY AFGHANISTAN's FAMILY SHIA STATUS LAW MUST BE CHANGED

By: Zareen Taj

My name is Zareen Taj and I am from Afghanistan. I am a women's rights/human rights activist, living in the United States. I have a B.S. in Political Science and Women's Studies, and a M.S. in Women's Studies. I am writing this letter to denounce parts of the Family Shia Status Law that was recently signed by President Karzai and is currently under review by the Ministry of Justice in Afghanistan. Parts of this law would adversely affect Hazara women. I am an Afghan woman, a Hazara woman and a Shia woman. I fall into all three categories that would be affected.

I draw my authority to speak from that fact and as my position as an insider of the Hazara Shia community. Reading the facts and consequences of this law has enraged me over about what is going on in Afghanistan and how the conservatives and extremists have found another way to oppress Hazara women. The west has only focused on the "marital rape" issue, not all the facts and consequences of this law.

This law has 250 restrictions on women. I have been in contact with Hazara women leaders and activists who have denounced this law. So my voice is the voice of all Hazara women in Afghanistan. This law violates the constitution of Afghanistan, which says women have equal rights and can be president. However, if a woman is not allowed to go out from her house, how possibly can she become president? How can she go to court when her rights are violated at home or she is being abused by her husband?

Family Shia Status Law

A part of the current Family Shia Status Law's stat ed intention was to regulate marriage, divorce, and inheritance issues for Afghanistan's Shia population. It should be noted that the country's Shia population represents approximately twenty percent of the total population. Of that twenty percent, ninety-five percent are the Hazara ethnic group. Sections of this law adversely affect the movement, rights, welfare and freedom of Hazara women.

The most restrictive sections of the law legislates the most intimate and personal family matters: in one section women are forbidden to leave the house without the husband's permission, he decides what are urgent or legitimate reasons; in another section women must wear makeup when asked by their husbands; in yet another section women are required to have sexual relations whenever the husband wants. There are many more unacceptable and controversial sections, all which conspire to keep the women prisoners in their homes and make them prisoners and slaves of the men.

Sections of this law are contrary to the Constitution of Afghanistan. Sections of this law erase the many gains that women have made these several years and the many rights that are enshrined in the constitution. Sections of this law tighten the yoke of oppression around the neck of Hazara women.

The main proponent behind this law is Sheikh Asef Mohseni. He has a dark past history of human rights violations. Mohseni pushed this law to please extremists and to move his political agenda forward. One of the results of this law will be an increasing hostility towards the Hazara community in general and Hazara women in particular.

Background on the Hazara in Afghanistan

The Hazara is a minority ethnic group in Afghanistan, which makes up the third largest ethnic group in present-day Afghanistan. Throughout their history, they have been the most persecuted, marginalized and oppressed ethnic group. There have been many wars and military campaigns to exterminate the Hazaras.

Some of these wars and campaigns are: Abdul Rahman's extermination campaigns in the 1880s and 1890s, which wiped out sixty-two percent of the Hazara population; the Afshar massacre in 1993 (over 1,000 killed); the Mazar-e Sharif massacre in 1998 (over 8,000 killed); Bamian massacres in 1998-99 and 2001; the Yakaolang massacres in 1999 and 2000.

The Taliban have targeted Hazaras for extinction because they considered them to be infidels. Their Mongol characteristics have made them distinct from the other ethnic groups and have caused them to be singled out for persecution. The Hazaras have been fighting for their very existence, rights, and identity for centuries. The history of Hazara has always been a history of suffering, a history of oppression and a history of struggle for existence and survival. This law continues that oppression.

Hazaras place the strongest value on education. Hazara people believe their survival is based on obtaining an education and freedom for women. Because of this value Hazara women have much freedom in their community to get an education, employment and to move freely without restriction from their homes and community in general. This law restricts their mobility and freedom.

Hazara Women Leaders

Within the Hazara community, the freedom, mobility and lack of restrictions have allowed women to participate in all walks of life. As a result, we have=2 0many Hazara women leaders and activists. For instance, the first head of the Women's Ministry was a Hazara woman; the first head of the Human Rights Commission is a Hazara woman; the first Governor of a province in Afghanistan is a Hazara woman; the first female Mayor in the country is a Hazara woman.

They have never received threats from Hazara men because of their position. In 2004, I went to Afghanistan for research and to make a documentary. As a Hazara woman I was welcomed by the Hazara people in Hazarajat. For over two months I never felt threatened. Nobody objected to my research or my crews with cameras. This law will prevent these accomplishments in the future.

Who supports this law?

The supporters of this law come from many interest groups. First, there are those who feel this law represents a form of Shia pride. Now mostly the illiterate and elders of Shia feel this law creates a Shia identity and provides recognition of their Shia religion in Afghanistan, which gives the m pride and identity.

They support this law because it is a Shia law, without knowing the entire law or the consequences of this law. Second, there are those who feel the law reinforces the classic patriarchal boundaries on women that have been eroding with their new found freedoms. Third, there are those who wish to advance their political agendas under the guise of "Shia Family law".

To challenge a religious law brings immediate condemnation and accusations of blasphemy and infidel. Fourth, there are those who feel that this law will silence any modern, progressive thinking and advancement. People are afraid and intimidated to speak out publically for fear of all kinds of retribution. This law will silence those individuals.

This specific support by these kinds of people and groups should be viewed as a red flag and a serious warning signal of the rapidly advancing attacks on women's freedoms. These warning signs represent a backward sliding into previous darkness and a silencing and censorship of those who would speak out in Afghanistan.

Why Karzai signed this law

I believe that when President Karzai signed this law, he has shown that he is taking this country in the wrong direction and does not support equality and freedom for women. When President Karzai signed this law, he did so in contradiction to Article 22 of the Afghan Constitution. When he signed this law he did so in contradiction to the International Convention on the Elimination of all Forms of Discrimination against Women, to which Afghanistan is a state party.

My question is "was President Karzai aware of the law's contents and consequences? He admitted that he signed this law without reading it. This shows how irresponsible he is toward our country and demonstrates that he just wanted to please the conservative mullahs to get their political support in the upcoming election.

Consequences of the law

The consequences of the law are many. First, it is a step backward for all women in Afghanistan. It is a double step back for Hazara women because they enjoy more freedom than most. Second, it is a threat to women' s freedom and mobility.

Third, it affects all Hazara women who are head of hous eholds. Fourth, it negatively affects all women's rights in divorce, child custody, marriage, and inheritance situations. Fifth, it allows a creeping "Talibanization" of society under the guise of "Shi'a family law. Sixth, it creates a triple oppression for Hazara women (gender, ethnic and religious discrimination). Seventh, it gives more freedom to extremists to oppress women without any restriction.

Conclusion

Finally, this law should be changed because of what it represents at its very core. It devalues women as human beings, patronizes them as if they were children, and continues a sanctioned system of male dominance. It is morally wrong, a stain on the ground of Afghanistan and has caused both outrage and embarrassment for us.

I speak for all Hazara women as I say emphatically and without reservation, we want the international community to hear our cries, recognize our struggles, and fight to deliver us from the effects of this oppressive law and what it represents. Hazara women want to have the freedom to utilize their talents.

We cannot do that with the restrictions of this law. The world should hear our voices as we demand that the government of Afghanistan change this law. Hazara women want to make it extremely clear, that the people who drafted this law do not and never will represent our community and values.

CHAPTER SEVEN

OPIUM: A SHAMEFUL PHENOMENON

By Jawad Rahmani

Recently, one of the friends and I were talking about challenges faced by Afghan people out of the country and how they are humiliated and discriminated on various basis. We talked much, and he shared his experiences in detail from which I found two vitally important to share with my readers, particularly Afghans. He is doing his masters in India and he has Asian face.

He was telling me that when people approached him and thought that he was somewhere from China or some East Asian countries, they were so amiable and friendly. "But, generally, such gentleness does not last long at a time when I am telling about my citizenship. Most of them just leave away or talk about Mullah Omer or Osama bin Laden".

The second thing he said was about his experience in Iran, when during Taliban regime he was forced to leave and seek refuge in neighbouring country. He told about several incidents when Iranians were abusing him and mocking him as an Afghani. "You are an Afghani boy, you smell opium and drugs." and then stopped him and were taking all his money in pocket and, ultimately, welcomed him by throwing several punches on his face.

This, of course, might look exaggeration for those who have not left the country or have not sought refuge. For Afghan refugees there, this piece of diary-like writing looks pity and ignorable. Their pain and sufferings dwarf, perhaps, terrible experiences they had during destructive civil war in their own country.

As some of you might have noted in above paragraphs two different things in two different countries. In India, it was all about terrorism and Al-Qaeda, particularly, its assassinated leader, Osama bin Laden and, while, in Iran it was about drug, narcotic and opium.

In another word, in Iran Afghan people are well-known because of drugs, while, in India, Afghan people are falsely linked to Osama bin Laden, because of his short-term settlement and launching the horrible 9/11 terror attacks from here, which shocked the world and built a notion that the headquarter of terror-networks were somewhere in Afghanistan. But why people of two different countries have different picture from Afghanistan and Afghan people.

Likely, these two different notions are linked to problems caused by these two dangerous phenomena. India has been a target of Terrorists and suffered much from activities of networks like that of Al-Qaeda.

However, several attacks were launched in Iran, but what has been growing as real danger there is opium and drugs exported from its neighbour. According to unofficial statistics, addiction has crossed a million and the number is increasingly growing larger and larger.

However, the government has strictly prohibited drug-usage; traffickers and smokers both are criminal according to country's ruling laws; but tangible success has not been achieved yet. Day by day, the law is getting stricter, and for those who carry few grams of drug, there is capital punishment, but still executed traffickers and carriers are replaced by new ones and drugs are exported from here across the world.

There are allegations that Iranian officials have been trying to employ a new measure to control drug trafficking: letting Afghan refugees get addicted and then force them to return to Afghanistan. However, there are no documents for the plan, but there is something noteworthy to mention.

Huge numbers of Afghan refugees in Iran suffer from addiction. Even young people, whom I know very well, migrated for seeking employment to Iran during Taliban regime and during post-Taliban period Iran and has returned with addiction.

In addition, the notion is further strengthened by putting a glimpse to condition of returned refugees in border province like Herat, where huge number of them walk purposelessly and engaged in small social crimes, like pick-pocketing.

As I said there are no documents for such a plan, but if there were really a plan, Tehran officials should not be blamed, because what they are doing is protecting citizen against a growing danger—addiction—which increases social crimes and destroys foundations of numerous families. Whatever helps bringing down the level of addiction among people, they would not leave undone and would apply to salvage their people.

No doubt, there are people across the world that is mad on us and telling that if there was not country like Afghanistan, their sons and daughters would have had better and dignified life. Arguing that, it is Afghanistan that produces over 90 percent of world opium.

It should be noticed that these people, unfortunately, ignoring some other realities. In other word, there is not only opium or its products' addiction. There are various types of addiction, taking from alcohol to marijuana. From total world addicts, only small portion of them are addicted to opium manufacturing from Afghanistan.

It does not mean I want to justify opium cultivation and production in Afghanistan. Frequently, I have shouted that this phenomenon is destructive and a shame for country as well as for people. It should be eliminated by any possible means. Unfortunately, it is widely cultivated still, because Kabul officials are involved too and are not serious to eradicate it.

Measures held till now, like distribution of improved wheat seeds and employing police force to destroy cultivated opium and etc, have not proved well. And there has also been a shameful silence from influential religious leaders and tribal heads. Here in Afghanistan, people are tight more than anything else with belt of community and religion.

If they hold Jihad and make sacrifices is largely because of religion. Religion is an absolute driving force and people would not cultivate opium if religious leaders stand seriously and clarify that opium cultivation is anti-Islam. But they have not yet, what they did was vague and folded advice from which people have got nothing of opium sin or illegality. (Daily Outlook Afghanistan).

Narcotics in Afghanistan: Dilawar Sherzai

The announcement by Deputy Interior Minister of Counter Narcotics on June 20, 2011, mentioning that over three million Afghans are involved in manufacturing or trafficking drugs, has further added concerns to the drug issue that has already been bothering the honest national and international counter narcotics efforts. Afghanistan is considered as the top producer of narcotics and the country has been suffering because of this menace for the last 35 years or so.

The first notable growth of poppy cultivation in Afghanistan can be traced in mid 70's. The Afghan government at that time was very weak, with partial control over the provinces which largely were under the control of landlords and depended highly on agriculture. The landlords were not under strict control of the central government regarding the production of their agricultural activities.

The demand of opium at that time was basically triggered by the fact that there was a ban going on in Iran regarding poppy cultivation. This made the landlords in

Afghanistan turn their attentions towards poppy cultivation and by the late 1970's almost half of Afghan provinces had started growing opium.

In 1978 Soviet Union invaded Afghanistan, and the first years of war mostly from 1979 to 1982 between the Soviet Union and the opposing groups, further deteriorated the situation of peace, harmony and stability. Invasion by Soviet Union turned the course of both national and international politics. The countries opposing Soviet Union, especially America, started supporting the opposing forces in Afghanistan, with the help of Afghan neighbouring countries.

The Jihadi networks in Afghanistan were basically strengthened during the same era to counter the atheist Soviet Union. This phenomenon started transfer of funds and supports in to the country that was then, to a considerable extent, used for the investment in the production and trafficking of narcotics.

Afghanistan turned into a giant producer and trafficker of opium with no prominent control. By the mid 1980's Afghanistan produced one third of the total global production of opium; a total of 800 metric tones. And they were administered by seven major Mujahedeen Groups.

In 1989 when Russia withdrew its forces out of Afghanistan, the Mujahedeen who were being supported militarily and financially by external forces had to face a decline in support. As a result, the Mujahedeen's had to dig out their own means of generating economic and military support for themselves.

But, as there were no other sources of generating income available in the country the dependence was further laid on poppy cultivation. By 1992, Mujahedeen took over Kabul, but not with a very strong central command, thus resulting into fragmentation of the county into many tribes and groups.

The individual warlords took no interest in strengthening the central government and each started living on his own. Again the only source that was available for their financial support was opium.

Thus, they did their best to provide the ever thirsty market with huge productions. By the mid 90's Afghanistan produced 2,200 to 2,400 metric tones of opium each year. The fragmentation of the country at the same time provided an opportunity to Taliban to seize power. In 1996, Taliban were able to gain control of most parts of the country and with a comparatively stronger central government in Kandahar.

The reign of Taliban further organized the narcotics industry, as they also had to generate resources for themselves after being left without proper support from their earlier supporters. Narcotics at that time became a part of organized crime in Afghanistan and better international connections were made available for its business.

In the first year of Taliban's reign, there was a considerable rise in the production. In 1997/98 total production was 2,700 metric tones, which was a 43% rise as compared to previous year. In 98/99 the production reached to its peak at 4,500 metric tones, representing three quarters of world supply. During the same era there was a draught in the country that reduced the food production to a very miserable extent.

As a result of this draught the country was further pushed towards illicit activities. Subsequently, Taliban initiated a ban on the production of opium, which had a considerable impact on the overall production and it reached to negligible amount. Only some areas outside the Taliban control continued the poppy cultivation.

The incident of 9/11 which resulted in the assault of Afghanistan by American forces in 2001 ended the control of Taliban in Afghanistan. The change in Afghanistan's political setup started with the agreement in the Bonn Conference in December 2001.

This transition reached to its required result in the parliamentary elections of 2005 that concluded with the formation of the interim government led by President Hamid Karzai. So much has been changed since the formation of this so called democratic government.

Now, the central government enjoys much authority extending to most of the corners of the country. The security arrangements have improved and the country is now having a comparatively stronger army and police and the administrative setup has improved much. All these have been possible with considerable support from foreign allies of Afghanistan.

But, it is unfortunate to note that the country has not made any considerable improvement regarding the eradication of opium production and its trafficking. Once again the country is standing among the leading producers and trafficker of opium, with the involvement of three million Afghans. And it is a government statistical record, there may be more involved in the process.

With the developments in all the other areas of the country, it is really unfortunate that there has been development in the industry of narcotics as well. The processes of production and smuggling of narcotics have turned complex. Now, it would not be sufficient to say that land lords are individually involved in the processes and the economic crisis is responsible for its opium production.

Rather the phenomenon has gone through considerable changes. Presently, this industry has become more consolidated, rather than its fragmented past. There are more organized groups participating in the processes rather than individual names.

It has become a part of more organized crime with the involvement of international mafia. And proper and more supportive backing is being provided to it from many culprits from within the government and international traders.

Therefore, in order to think of any proper solution of the issue the complexities related to the phenomenon has to be understood properly. Only the formation of anti-narcotics force can not solve the issue. There has to be both international and national initiatives in this regard, with proper accountability and punishment of those who are wolves in sheep clothing among the concerned authorities. And above all, all the initiatives must be pursued with honest intentions.

Rising Drug Addiction Deadlier Than War

According to the Ministry of Counter Narcotics, now and with the prices of opium going back up, more land might be used for cultivation and the production is set to return to previous levels if the anti-poppy campaign is not intensified and farmers are not presented with viable alternatives.

There has been an explosion in the number of drug-addicts in the country in recent years. The human casualties of the sprawling drug production in our country are no longer confined to the streets of Tehran, Moscow or London. An increasing number of our own fellow Afghans are being hooked to opium, heroin and hashish.

When the government of Afghanistan and its supporting partners still struggle to provide basic healthcare facilities to teeming masses of impoverished people, they will inevitably attach less importance to providing treatment and support to this growing opiate-addict population.

In the midst of a social and economic breakdown, the level of drug addiction in the country is sure to rise further if the government and its international supporters do not mobilize required resources to tackle the plague as addressing the issue is urgent. They say one stitch in time saves nine. We do not expect our under-resourced government, as it stands now, to save all the nine. Saving even one would be a golden achievement.

CHAPTER EIGHT

AFGHANISTAN'S KIDNAPPING AND WEAPON INDUSTRY

Don't go to Afghanistan if you want to save money. These are the words of one of my journalist friends who recently described a frightening story of kidnapping for ransom and illegal weapon business. Kidnapping for ransom and smuggling of weapons from Central Asia has been a profitable business in Afghanistan since the fall of the Taliban regime in 2001.

Some under ground group, who enjoy the protection of some Afghan police and intelligence officials and private militias across the country, pick up men, women and children one by one either for the purposes of human trafficking, organ business or for ransom business. These groups enjoy the protection of Taliban and neighbouring states who want the fulfilment of their agenda through this business.

The international aspect of this business is that some states don't want the involvement of their political and geographical enemy states to be involved in the reconstruction of Afghanistan; they are supporting the kidnapping and killing of workers of some reconstruction companies. Criminal are experienced and trained people and the last thing they want is shots fired in the middle of the night.

Last year, two men working for a local NGO were kidnapped by unknown criminals during a community meeting. Later on, an innocent British woman was kidnapped and killed in Kunar province. The political influence of these gangs is also an important dynamic.

As these groups enjoy the protection of corrupt police officials who are their business partners as well , some corrupt Afghan intelligence officials who not only receive their share; they receive a lot of money from the Taliban in exchange of sensitive and secret information protect these people. Corrupt elements in the Afghan intelligence have been involved in the illegal businesses of weapons and the business of China White Heroin.

Kidnapping and illegal drug business is a most powerful industry in today Afghanistan. Members of Afghan parliament have deeply been involved in this profitable business since 1990s. Kidnappings are common in many parts of Afghanistan. When US invaded the country, kidnappings were rare and mostly politically motivated.

The average ransom was a hefty sum to many Afghans, $10,000. In 2011, the rate reached to 200,000 US dollars. Consequently, these criminals became influential land mafia launched the kidnapping business, use their purchased empty houses and plazas as temporary prisons for their victims.

There are also strong links among the Tajik and Uzbek Islamist insurgent groups and the Afghan weapons and drug smugglers, some officials alleged. "We share porous borders with Tajikistan and Uzbekistan which are used by some subversive elements to smuggle weapons, drugs and other illegal items," Once smuggled from Tajikistan and other countries, the weapons quickly find their way to the volatile south and south-eastern provinces.

Here again, accusations are strong against security forces, government officials and local strongmen for their alleged involvement and support in the domestic transport and the smuggling of weapons. It is believed that some smuggling networks even operate in an environment of criminal impunity owing to their alleged ties with senior government officials.

These hard-core criminal elements from different political and sectarian groups, hired by land mafia to protect their embezzled estates have started settling down in urban areas, and have polluted the local scenario with their criminal activities.   They enjoy readymade facilities to carry out their illegal business.

These religious and political mafia groups making million dollars from the illicit drug trade, security charges of convoys, extortions and financial contributions from charities and wealthy individuals from various Arab States.

The business of kidnap for ransom support terrorist Taliban in both Pakistan and Afghanistan. Afghan and Pakistan criminals groups involved in kidnapping for ransom in Afghanistan, Punjab, Khyber Pakhtunkhwa and Baluchistan are financially aiding the Afghan and Pakistani Taliban networks. In Punjab, one of my friend police officer told me in a telephonic conversation that some 100 to 150 people are being kidnapped in the province every month.

"We have reports that groups involved in ransom business have links with the Taliban of Waziristan- and Afghanistan-based militants, he told me. These underground and over-ground groups have spawned an epidemic of ransom kidnappings. Once, Asia Times reported the abduction of some 237 people from different parts of Baluchistan in 2010.

In the Afghan capital, over one hundred people are being kidnapped every month. These criminal who enjoy the support of Taliban as well, killed many captives while demands for ransom went unmet. We still remember the brutal killing of a British woman kidnapped for ransom in 2011, because most criminal groups' kidnappings end either in the payment of a ransom or the death of the hostage.

The money these groups earn from this business goes into the pockets of four category people. The first group is Taliban who help them in kidnapping local and foreigners, the second is the corrupt officials of the Afghan police, the third is elements in the Afghan intelligence and the fourth group that receive its share is private warlords' militias.

One another formidable aspect of the business is that as these groups belong to sectarian and political parties of Afghanistan they spend a lot of money on the purchase of weapons from a cross Central Asia and Iran.

Some Afghan experts are of the opinion that several ethnic and sectarian groups of the country distribute sophisticated weapons among their member for future civil war after the NATO and US withdrawal in 2014. Some military experts understand that the weapons they purchase go into the hands of Pakistani Taliban group. Two months ago, armed criminals kidnapped 12 Iranian engineers from western Afghanistan for ransom.

Heartbreaking reports recently revealed about the illegal weapon business in Northern Afghanistan. Local criminals, police and intelligence officials are jointly running the profitable business of sophisticated weapons in Kunduz, Mazar-e-Sharif, Herat, Takhar, Balkh Samangan, Parwan and Baghlan provinces.

A police commander from Afghanistan told me that smugglers use the Darqad Pass between Tajikistan and the northern Afghan province of Takhar for weapon smuggling. "The connection between smugglers, terrorism, the Taliban and al-Qaeda indicates that they bring arms from Pakistan and provide them to terrorists and Taliban," Deputy Head of Counternarcotics Department General Baz Mohammad Ahmadi said.In the past one month seven Iranian citizens have been detained on charges of cross-border drug smuggling, officials said.

"The problem is we have not enough equipment and personnel and our borders are open; other countries like Islamic Republic of Iran have no such problems," General Ahmadi said."I regret that such amount of weapons and chemicals could be transported into Afghanistan. If a lorry loaded with chemicals crosses into Afghanistan without being caught on the heavily-guarded Iranian borders, it makes us be suspicious that there has been some sort of settlements with Iranian customs department and border forces."

What is said to be the involvement of low-level Afghan officials in drug smuggling has made the counternarcotics more difficult. "There has been no pressure from higher and minister levels for release of smugglers, but it has been at governor and council member levels," General Ahmadi said.

Around 120 operations have been conducted nationwide in the past one month and more than 3,100kg of opium, 1,700kg of heroin and 7kg of morphine and some other kinds of drugs have been seized, according to the department. More than 800 acres of land have been cleared of poppy and around 170 suspects have been arrested in connection with drug related activities, it said.

Weapons smuggling into Afghanistan is increasing, the United Nations representative said on Monday, expressing concern about violence in the country. Tom Koenigs said he did not know where the arms came from and where they went but said they were an 'expression of insecurity'.

"I have got some information that the weapons smuggling into Afghanistan is increasing," he told reporters. "We have already far too many weapons in this country even without this smuggling."

"It is certainly one expression of the insecurity in this country that people turn to weapons," he said.

"The exchange of arms for heroin makes a lot of money – more than we get from heroin smuggling alone," said Mir Alam. "Each time the weapons are exchanged for heroin, both sides get a profit from both arms and heroin. It's a good trade. I know people who have luxury palaces in Dubai and other Arab countries thanks to this trade."

The major profits go to those with the clout to call on adequate protection. "The big smugglers are backed by governments in Afghanistan, Pakistan and Central Asia," he said. "These smugglers can pay huge amounts of money. But we don't do badly."

On the other side of the border, heroin is smuggled further into Tajikistan, and from there through the Central Asian republics to Russian and European markets. The trade generates large profits along its way, although not so much for those who simply ferry it across the Tajik-Afghan border.

"We really don't make that much money out of this," said one Tajik smuggler. "Our job is just to get the sacks of heroin across the border, then the Russian mafia come with their vehicles, many of which have police insignia. They take the heroin and give us the guns. Then they take the drugs to Europe.

"All along the way we bribe the police. The Russians do, too, but they have to give money to high-ranking officials. Failing that, it's impossible."

In past years, Badakhshan mostly grew, processed and exported its own opium, the raw material of heroin. Now, given the explosion of cultivation in the south, especially in Helmand, and a largely successful eradication process in Badakhshan itself, the Northern Province has become a clearing-house for drugs from other provinces.

One resident of Ishkashim district of Afghan Badakhshan, speaking on condition of anonymity, was happy to guide a visitor through the process by which raw opium is turned into heroin.

"I have been running a small heroin-processing lab for three years now," he said. "My brothers and partners, however, are mostly involved in smuggling, because it gives them a lot of income."

They smuggle heavy weapons such as rockets and mortars mostly at night. A source in Afghan interior Ministry told me that police vehicles are being used narco and weapon smuggling across the country. During the last thirty years of civil war in Afghanistan, huge demand foe modern weapons were created and now many armed actors which seek political, economic and other interests through armed violence.

Military relations among Afghan separatists and Tajik and Uzbek Islamist insurgent from Central Asia are too friendly. Afghanistan shares porous borders with Tajikistan and Uzbekistan which are used by some subversive elements to smuggle weapons into the country.

The announcement of President Obama about the withdrawal of US troops from Afghanistan created a lot of guesswork in Kabul. As no specific military, economic and political progress has taken roots during the last ten years presence of international community, the country will remain vulnerable to insurgent groups before and after their withdrawal in 2014. This premature disengagement will leave profound consequences for the future of Afghanistan.

Taliban have not been defeated and al Qaeda is still there. Afghan citizens, including parliamentarians and military establishment are bewildered that foreign forces are leaving with fighting still raging.

The US and its allies failed to adequately resource the Afghan campaign. Military spending on private criminal militias or Blackwater though increased in the number of irregular warriors but led to huge waste, inflation and corruption. This irregular spending increased the cost of war and damaged the reputation of the Afghan Government.

Millions of Afghans continues to suffer from shortages of housing, clean water, electricity, medical care, and jobs. Afghan National Army still has many weaknesses, fully dependent on embedded trainers and regretfully, still, not able to effectively tackle insurgency in the country. Warlords and mafia groups started reorganization of their forces while in the government circles; American friends are mournful and say they are being left helpless.

Interestingly, President Obama in his announcement did not include any long-term commitment like that offered to Japan and Korea decades ago. This created more distrust about the future of US-Afghan friendship.

Afghanistan already troubled by major societal and economic problems, especially, vulnerable to additional challenges posed by the influx of arms from Central Asia. Over the last ten years due to insufficient investment poverty has become more concerning as the rate of unemployment is rapidly rising.

As the country has become known as a guaranteed stock of sophisticated arms and drug for war criminals and Taliban, the cloud of civil war are re-appearing within the Afghan frontiers with a heavy rain of bullets.

The vast majority of Afghan arms are going into the streets of black market. The Afghan poor stockpile security and mismanagement has made arms depots attractive to smugglers and vulnerable to loss. Weapons of these depots are secretly going into the hands of smugglers and end up in the hands of Pakistani and Afghani Taliban groups.

In many occasions, arms and ammunition have been stolen or looted in various provinces of the country or Afghan police and National Army soldiers sold these weapons for cash. In Afghanistan, as army personnel are not properly paid for their services, they have no option to cooperate with insurgents for cash and supply them with weapons in exchange of money.

There are documented cases of Afghan soldiers selling weapons to Taliban fighters. Not only the smuggling of weapons become a profitable business in Afghanistan, the trafficking of drugs, timber, diamonds and even the smuggling of human beings is a popular trade. The militarization of crime in Afghanistan has become a threat not only to the state but also put in danger the security establishment of the country as well.

Having streamlined their business, Afghan arms traffickers mostly rely on various arm smuggling networks in Tajikistan, Iran, Pakistan and black markets in the region. In some provinces of the country, weapons are being bartered for hostages and heroin. Many Afghans ask who are these arms smugglers and from where they operate?

The answer in clear that during the Soviet intervention, international community and Pakistan utilized private arms brokers to facilitate Afghans in their struggle. These arms smugglers, however, deeply involved even after the Cold War ended, and the arms pipelines they had built remained operational to this day.

The horses of war criminals, drug mafia and private contractor are being prepared for a crucial race in the coming civil war that will drag Afghanistan back into fifteenth century ignorance. After the withdrawal of international coalition from Afghanistan, the country might slide back into war and renewed turmoil.

The business of kidnapping is in progress and every group want to collect a lot of money for financing their militarization process. Lists of business men, big shopkeepers, plazas owner, jewellers and landlords have reached the headquarters of criminal mafia groups. The root of all evils in Afghanistan is the 'worse security' that hampers all sorts of social, political and economic developments.

Political actors, former warlords and sectarian elements have started visiting the capitals of neighbouring states including India and Russia to take direction for the coming race in Afghanistan.

Those secretly associated with SCO have their own agendas. In Islamabad these days, Afghan tribal and political players booked cool rooms in luxury hotels, visiting bureaucrats, military generals and clerics for joining their race for political power in near future.

Islamabad has tired now because neither stability comes to Afghanistan nor Americans want to leave Pakistan alone. In June 2011, General Kiyani unwillingly told European delegation that: "Pakistan wants a stable Afghanistan but not at the cost of Pakistan," ignoring strategic depth he said that Islamabad wants to remain relevant in any peace initiative and is unlikely to accept a solution that would undermine its strategic interests.

Pakistan Interior Minister Rehman Malik demanded that the weapon smuggling issue must be resolved with Afghanistan as illegally imported arms were being used in terror incidents in Pakistan. He told reporters that terrorism could not be countered in a more effective way until and unless smuggling of weapons from Afghanistan was not stopped.

"Pakistan wants support from Afghanistan to eliminate terrorism from the region," he said. Commenting on prevailing situation in Karachi, he said that the government was committed to restoring peace in the provincial capital of Sindh. To a question, the interior minister said that no operation was going on in Karachi neither the government has any intention to take such initiative.

The Chief of Jamhoori Watan Party, Sardar Talal Bugti told reporters that the smuggling of arms and ammunition from Afghanistan to Pakistan was deep conspiracy by enemies to create bad law and order situation. He said that he contacted several times for meeting with the Chief of Army Staff and Chief of ISI to inform them about the conspiracies against the country but they do not had time to listen him.

He said that the anti state elements wanted to break the country and it was time for politicians and patriots to come forward and combat against their enemies. He said that the meeting of former president Musharraf was not co-incidental.

A news report in the Frontier Post (July 30, 2011) revealed that federal government was contemplating a programme to recover illegal arms and ammunition from all over the country to improve law and order. Sources said provincial heads will soon be asked to get ready for a crackdown on illegal arms holders and smugglers. According to interior ministry sources, the country has a huge quantity of illicit weapons.

Our enemies are cashing in on the Karachi situation and lurking all the time to weaken Pakistan, sources said. They maintained that owing to war efforts in Afghanistan, previous governments could not pay required attention to check arms smuggling into the country but the present government was taking all possible measures for prevention of arms smuggling and recovery of illegal arms in the country.

Before launching the drive, sources said, people would be appealed to step forward and identify elements with illegal arms or involved in arms smuggling. Sources maintained that heavy cash prizes would be given to officers who recovered illegal arms. The newspaper reported.

Some weapons, along with other military-issue supplies, are also being seized by Taliban militants in attacks on NATO convoys passing through Pakistan on their way to resupply soldiers in Afghanistan. Although such raids have been taking place for years [3], the Pakistani Taliban appear to have widened the zone where they are willing to operate, attacking NATO trucks in major cities as well, including in the capital of Islamabad as recently as June 9 [4].

An estimated one-third of the supplies bound for U.S. and NATO troops in Afghanistan travel by land from Pakistan's port city of Karachi. Pakistani intelligence officials said that, in many cases, the drivers moving the NATO containers are working with the Pakistani Taliban, which torches the containers after seizing the loaded goods.

Major General Ather Abbas, a spokesman for the Pakistan army, told Global Post that the U.S. weapons are being used by the Taliban against Pakistani forces in various tribal areas, including Bajaur, Mohmand and Khyber agencies, where militants have mounted a strong resistance to ongoing military operations.

The main problem in Afghanistan is money, if you have money this would amount to an open invitation to kidnappers in the current climate. Business men in the country have sent their children and families to UK and U.S and they are obliged to stay behind because of their business.

Police in Afghanistan accept that there has been an increase in kidnappings for ransom while business community are naturally concerned for their security. Justice system in the country has collapsed or infected with corruption and traditional politics.

All institutions are corrupt; there is no punishment for influential criminals. Criminal culture, insecurity, and the Afghan Government's inability to extend rule of law to all parts of the country pose challenges to future economic growth.

Afghan citizens understand that the government is a large part of the problem as the state police support criminals. For example an Afghan business man told reporters that once driving home from work in evening, he noticed that some criminals were following him, he called the police. When he got out of the car, masked men attacked him and tried to kidnap him but the police were helplessly waiting and the kidnappers fled.

CHAPTER NINE

THE QUESTION OF ISAF ELEVEN THOUSANDS MISSING CONTAINERS, PUNJABI TALIBAN AND BLA

The scam of ISAF's 11000 weapon loaded missing container has raised many questions that whether these missing containers were off loaded in Karachi, diverted to the headquarters of Punjabi Taliban in Bahawalpur, Southern Punjab or looted by the BLA? These questions have become much irksome to the law enforcement agencies and military establishment fighting insurgencies across the country.

The biggest scam of Pakistan's history and the missing of such a huge number containers containing weapons, whisky, military uniform and other prohibited and non-prohibited luggage has created the climate of fear and harassment across the country that lest these lethal weapons fall in the hands of Punjabi Taliban or invisible terror army in Karachi.

Federation of American Scientists has recently released a detailed report and identified important factors that gave rise to the threat of jihadist Taliban inside the country. Military-grade weapons FAS says are available to them in major towns and cities in all parts of FATA and Khyber Pakhtunkhwa.

It means the so-called Pakistani nuclear threat is only a pretext; Pakistan is the real target - owing to its role in complex US-China geopolitical relations. Writing in the Cutting Edge Magazine, (June 22nd 2011The) Shoshana Bryen revealed that CIA has been using drones in Pakistan from bases in Afghanistan because the US doesn't want to wage war in Pakistan from Pakistan, CIA wants to wage Pakistan's war from Afghanistan.

Moreover, there are signals indicating that failure to win the war against Taliban could tempt NATO to broaden the theatre of war into Pakistan. The danger is real and notwithstanding President Obama's assurance about the friendly ties with Pakistan, the United States is changing its stance on partnership with the country and creates a new issue of distrust every week.

In case of NATO military operation in Pakistan, an addition to the Afghan and Pakistani Taliban, the alliance would be facing five hundred thousands professional and well organised army. The recent threatening statement of General Petraeus to undertake unilateral military operations inside Pakistan was followed by NATO violations of Pakistan's airspace in North Waziristan. All these challenges faced by Pakistan are linking with the availability of military grade weapon to insurgents and terror groups.

On July 15, 2011, I came across a report of Pakistan's Federal Tax Ombudsman (January 2011) on the issue of ISAF's missing containers. This is a comprehensive report which gives readers a lot of information but only represents the Government of Pakistan's standpoint.

In my telephone conversation with one of a senior advisor of Federal Tax Ombudsman in Islamabad, he told me that since ISAF's Forward Mounting Base in Karachi was shifted to Kabul, coordination mechanism between the custom authorities and ISAF representative undermined.

He told me that this is the biggest scam of customs reported in country's history worth over Rs 220 billion Rupees. After the NLC, Hajj, Steel Mills, Rental Power Plants, Railway, PIA, KESC, and hundred other scandals, this scandal joins the series of high level corruption in Pakistan.

According to Pakistan's Federal Board of Revenue and customs intelligence sources in Lahore, these missing containers were imported to supply weapons to NATO in Afghanistan disappeared abruptly. Who received these containers and lethal weapons, who sold it to whom, nobody knows.

But the question is why Pakistan's over fifty intelligence agencies have so for been failed in recovering this huge number of weapon loaded containers or why they haven't carried out a thorough investigation into the scam?

Counter terrorism authorities in Islamabad understand that these weapon loaded missing containers might cause more violence across the country if these weapons fall into the hands of Punjabi Taliban, invisible armies in Karachi or Baloch National Army. Counter insurgency experts say, it will take Pakistan at lest a decade tackling multi faceted insurgencies across the country.

Interior Minister Mr. Rehman Malik revealed that police and security agencies recovered Israeli weapon from criminals, involved in target killings in Karachi. While making this startling disclosure, Interior Minister said that this development now crystal clearly proves that there are foreign hands behind the extreme unrest and state of emerging destabilization in Karachi, Pakistan financial capital and hub of country's economic and trade activities.

It appears that for the first time in past many years, Mr. Malik wanted to name a particular country; of course India for being behind weaponization and instability in Pakistan but deliberately avoided it in the backdrop of ongoing peace process between India and Pakistan, however naming India's closed ally Israel for the same was ultimately like putting an indirect finger towards RAW of India.

"Weapons are being brought to Karachi from abroad," he said, adding: "Not only weapons even target killers also were coming from outside." He said steps are being taken to tackle the situation but did not elaborate. "Over 200 persons have been arrested and Israel-made weapons, including AK-45s, have been recovered from them.

This proves that a foreign hand is behind the unrest in Karachi," he told newsmen here. The minister did not directly blame Israel for the Karachi turmoil. Israeli weapons had been injected in the 1980s during the Afghan Jihad against the Soviet intervention in Afghanistan.

Rehman Malik claimed that the law and order situation in Karachi would be brought under control soon. "President Asif Ali Zardari has ordered that peace should be restored in Karachi at any cost," he said

It remains a fact that in past; at many occasions Pakistan had claimed that its security agencies had recovered Arms and ammunition of Indian origin from different disturbed parts of the country. In that case it had become highly pivotal for Indian agencies to avoid supplying Indian weapons to their Pakistani operatives and instead opted for Israeli cooperation this time.

It is really matter of great surprise that suddenly the Israeli weapons have found a great deal of buyers in Pakistani underworld arms markets which clearly impossible if the shipments are not made via India and through the Indians.

In fact this phenomenon is not limited to Karachi but the whole of Pakistan and particularly in Baluchistan and more than that in FATA, these weapons have been smuggled in and distributed to keep the pot boiling. Some senior government functionaries including former KP Governor Owais Ahmad Ghani had openly stated that every bullet and every gun being used by the anti-State elements was being smuggled from Afghanistan.

There are strong reasons why Islamabad should look at India for the terror wave inside Pakistan. It is strange why Mr. Malik won't consider this possibility. His position becomes more untenable considering how his pro-US government has been reluctant to confront Washington and New Delhi on issues pertaining to Pakistan's legitimate interests.

The position of Karachi's largest political party MQM and its UK-based chief Altaf Hussain is worse. His support for the military operation against terrorists on Pakistan's border with Afghanistan should be appreciated. But Mr. Hussain has been exploiting recent terror attacks to get back at his political opponents.

Mr. Hussain's city has seen Indian-instigated terrorism over the years. But MQM chief never once criticized India for its meddling inside Pakistan, not even when Pakistani intelligence officials confronted Washington recently with evidence of Indian terrorism.

One is justified to question how these weapons are being freely brought, stored and distributed in the presence of not in hundreds but in thousands of security posts. The unchecked inflow of arms means that our borders are either not fully guarded or there are elements who allow the movements of arms under threats or after getting handsome reward and the law enforcement agencies have been unable to identify the smuggling routes.

Huge resources are being spent on those who have been given security responsibilities and there must be a proper system to monitor inflow of such deadly consignments. Reverting back to Karachi, the Israeli weapons do not necessarily reflect the fact that Israel itself is involved in disturbances.

Moreover, in India, an Army Court of Inquiry (CoI) indicted 27 Army officers for illegal sale of weapons for private use and recommended disciplinary proceedings against them. According to the Indian media, the army ordered a CoI under the then South Western Commander Lt Gen C K S Sabu to probe the allegations.

They said if found guilty the officers in the rank of Colonels and Lieutenant Colonels may also face the prospect of being tried by a General Court Martial (GCM). Summary of evidence proceedings have also been completed in some of the cases.

Some military experts in Islamabad understand that the disappearance of these weapon loaded containers has put the national security in a constant danger. The terror militia, despite being surrounded from all sides in Pakistan by Pakistani soldiers, continues to receive state of the art weapons, ammunition, fuel and funding, all from Afghanistan.

When Pakistanis confronted senior US military and intelligence officers about this, their answer was that the money is coming from the drug trade controlled by the Afghan Taliban and that the advanced US-made weapons in the hands of the Pakistani Taliban, used to kill Pakistanis, were stolen from the US-trained Afghan National Army.

Pakistan Naval Station (PNS) Mehran is located in Karachi, in the southern Sindh province. Karachi has not endured the same degree of militancy as other parts of the country, though it has not been unscathed. The assault on Mehran is seen by many experts as deeply embarrassing for Pakistan.

The assault by Pakistani militants on the naval air station at Mehran in Karachi represents a highly sophisticated attack against an important military installation.
The base is home to Pakistan's US-supplied Orion P3-C maritime patrol aircraft. At least two of the aircraft were destroyed.

A few US contractors - as well as a small number of Chinese engineers - were also at the base. Their presence highlights the peculiar split nature of Pakistan's military alliances.

The attack, audacious by the standards of Pakistan's Taliban, raises all sorts of awkward questions about security at the facility. Did standards just slip? Were the militants underestimated? And what does it imply for security at other key installations, not least those associated with Pakistan's nuclear deterrent?

The Karachi project is the terror nexus named after the Pakistani port city and crime capital where Indian criminal dons like Dawood Ibrahim and Tiger Memon have been housed. The so called "joint-venture" between the terrorist groups and criminal networks was conceived some time after 2003 under the' criminal-terrorism fusion model' and has been supported by the state.

Daily Times (February 18, 2011), reported Pakistan's parliament Standing Committee serious reservations and pressure on Defence Minister and Chairman Federal Board of Revenue to explain the Government stance.

The committee was told that only 7000 containers were missing which is not true. The Committee asked about the agreement between Pakistan and NATO Alliance which allowed the NATO-ISAF containers to pass through Pakistan without scrutiny.

In response to the Supreme Court and public allegations, Federal Tax Ombudsman (FTO) prepared a detailed report on the missing of NATO weapon loaded containers. The report accepts the inabilities of the Custom Officials.

Moreover, following the report revelations, Government of Pakistan suspended 22 officials of the Pakistan Customs Service for their involvement in the container scandal.

According to Pakistan's think Tank report, since the commencement of Operation Enduring Freedom in Afghanistan, Pakistan allowed more than 300,000 NATO containers to pass from Karachi to Afghanistan through Chamman or Torkhum Border. During the Musharaf regime, Pakistani officials had no authority to even scan the containers.

The main hurdle here is that US military cargos carry Radio Frequency Identification Devices which gives the sole right of monitoring to American Homeland Security, no Pakistani agency or institution has access to these containers.

The US government doesn't share this with other partners. More importantly, more than eighty percent of military cargoes are being handled by ISAF and NATO hired private companies. The suspected threat arises from the delay of the containers.

For example, NATO containers need the certificate of Afghan embassy crossing the border and it may take 15 days. Pakistani officials are of the opinion that in this relatively long space of time most of the containers are changed, altered or emptied.

The biggest problem faced by Pakistan is the smuggling of arms within the country through these suspected containers. Media reports have already highlighted the suspected movement of these containers carrying arms through false declaration or fake documents. Military experts in Islamabad say these containers are enough for sustaining Taliban or Baloch insurgents for a decade.

The general situation in Afghanistan not only is not fully stable but also is deteriorating, reflecting a fluid political and military environment. Afghan government has failed in its attempt to assert control over the country characterized by over two decades of war, natural disaster and instability. In the constellation of political structures of Afghanistan, the Taliban are emerging as prominent corporate entity.

A Supreme Court bench, headed by Chief Justice Iftikhar Mohammad Chaudhry, had taken notice of the import of contraband items under the garb of food supplies meant for the International Security Assistance Force (Isaf) in Afghanistan.

The chief justice observed that the scandal involving the customs department had caused a huge loss of about Rs37 billion. He said the court had gone through the comprehensive report on smuggling of foreign goods in the name of ATT.

The National Logistic Cell started ISAF transit in May 2002 but did not ensure scanning and tracking mechanisms on transport being authorised by it to private transporters for transit cargo. "Indeed, the existing precautionary measures are too porous to be effective against organised fraud and manipulation."

The report highlighted the presence of an environment where dubious customs officials, clearing agents and businessmen colluded with each other. "In a world dominated by white-collar crime, the syndicates use expertise, knowledge, financial resources and contacts to hatch plots to loot the biggest bank of the country — the state treasury.

A three-member bench of the apex court, comprising Chief Justice Iftikhar Muhammad Chaudhry, Justice Tariq Parvez and Justice Ghulam Rabbani, was hearing the bail application of driver of container loaded with foreign liquor bottles. The court also clubbed all the cases of such nature and directed Muneer Qureshi, Member Customs, to submit his statement over the episode on September 23, satisfying the questions and concerns raised by the court.

ISAF's Forward Mounting Base (FMB) established at Karachi in early 2002 started its import procedures well by instituting an appropriate coordination mechanism by designating one of its officers at Karachi to regularly coordinate Customs clearance matters with Additional Collector Customs, Karachi Airport. But this coordination system fizzled out once the FMB was shifted by ISAF to Kabul within a year of its establishment at Karachi.

Had FBR demanded continuation of the effective arrangement for coordination with ISAF HQ Kabul through alternate nomination of a Karachi based official representative as has been put in place now, after the 'ISAF Scam' came to light, the possibilities of misuse of ISAF transit facility would have been contained.

Yet another serious dimension of mishandling the transport coordination by NLCis that NLC itself being a bonded carrier was required to have tracking system for live monitoring of the vehicles movement. Being fully aware of this condition, NLC should not have authorized private sector transport that did not have state of the art tracking system fitted in their vehicles to operate

CHAPTER TEN

WOMEN RIGHTS IN ISLAM

With the advent of Islam came the verse from the Quran condemning those who practiced female infanticide: "And when the news of (the birth of) a female (child) is brought to any of them, his face becomes dark, and he is filled with inward grief! He hides himself from the people because of the evil of that whereof he has been informed. Shall he keep her with dishonour or bury her in the earth? Certainly, evil is their decision."(An-Nahl 16:58-59).

On the Day of Judgment, the Quran mentions: "And when the female (infant) buried alive (as the pagan Arabs used to do) shall be questioned. For what sin she was killed? (At-Takwir 81:8-9).

Allah (J) says in the Holy Quran: "O You who believes! You are forbidden to inherit women against their will, and you should not treat them with harshness, that you may take away part of the Mahr (bridal-money given by the husband to his wife at time of marriage) you have given them, unless they commit open illegal sexual intercourse. And live with them honourably. If you dislike them, it may be that you dislike a thing and Allah brings through it a great deal of good." (An-Nisa 4:19.)

In another verse, Allah (J) says: "O mankind! Be dutiful to your Lord, Who created you from a single person (Adam), and from him (Adam) He created his wife (Eve), and from them both He created many men and women and fear Allah through Whom you demand your mutual (rights), and (do not cut the relations of) the wombs (kinship). Surely, Allah is Ever and All-Watcher over you." (Al-Nisa 4:1)

Hazrat Muhammad (S) said: "Assuredly, women are the twin halves of men." (Sahih reported by Abu-Dawud (RA). According to the Holy Quran: "Then Satan whispered suggestions to them both in order to uncover that which was hidden from them of their private parts (before); he said: "Your Lord did not forbid you this tree save you should become angels or become of the immortals." And he (Satan) swore by Allah to them both (saying): "Verily, I am one of the sincere well-wishers for you both." So he misleads them with deception. Then when they tasted of the tree, that which was hidden from them of their shame (private parts) became manifest to them and they began to stick together the leaves of Paradise over themselves (in order to cover their shame). And their Lord called out to them (saying): "Did I not forbid you that tree and tell you: Verily, Satan is an open enemy unto you?" They said: "Our Lord! We have wronged ourselves. If you forgive us not, and bestow not upon us Your Mercy, we shall certainly be of the losers." (Allah) said: "Get down, one of you an enemy to the other (i.e. Adam, Eve, and Satan, etc.). On earth will be a dwelling-place for you and an enjoyment, - for a time." He said: "Therein you shall live, and therein you shall die, and from it you shall be brought out (i.e. resurrected)."(Al-A'raf 7:20-25)

About the civil rights of a Muslim woman the Quran says: (O Mankind! We have created you from a male and a female, and made you into nations and tribes, that you may know one another. Verily, the most honourable of you in the Sight of Allah is the believer who has Taqwa (piety and righteousness). Verily, Allah is All-Knowing, All-Aware.)[49:13]. Allah, the Exalted and Almighty, states in the Glorious Qur'an: (O mankind! Be dutiful to your Lord, Who created you from a single person (Adam), and from him (Adam) He created his wife (Eve), and from them both He created many men and women...) [4:1].

Allah(J) also says in the Holy Quran: (Does man think that he will be left neglected without being punished or rewarded for the obligatory duties enjoined by his Lord (Allah) on him? Was he not a mixed male and female discharge of semen pouring forth? Then he became a clot; then (Allah) shaped and fashioned (him) in due proportion, and made him into two sexes, male and female. Is He not able to raise to life those who are dead?), [75:36-40].

In Dr. Muhammad Sharif Chaudhry book (Women Rights in Islam); he has quoted the following verses of the Holy Quran and Hadeiths regarding the rights in Islam:

1. Permitted to you, on the night of the fasts, is the approach to your wives. They are your garments and ye are their garments. Allah knoweth what ye used to do secretly among yourselves: But He turned to you and forgave you:(2:187)

2. Your wives are as a tilth unto you: so approach your tilth when or how ye will: but do some good act for your souls beforehand; and fear Allah, and know that ye are to meet Him (in the Hereafter) and give (these) good tidings to those who believe. (2:223)

3. And women shall have rights similar to the rights against them, according to what is equitable; but men have a degree (of advantage) over them. And Allah is exalted in Power, Wise. (2:228)

4. A divorce is only permissible twice: after that, the parties should either hold together on equitable terms or separate with kindness. It is not lawful for you, (men), to take back any of your gifts (from your wives) except when both parties fear that they would be unable to keep the limits ordained by Allah. If ye (judges) do indeed fear that they would be unable to keep the limits ordained by Allah, there is no blame on either of them if she gives something for her freedom. These are the limits ordained by Allah; so do not transgress them. If any do transgress the limits ordained by Allah, such persons wrong (themselves as well as others). (2:229)

5. There is no blame on you if ye divorce women before consummation or the fixation of their dower: but bestow on them (a suitable gift) the wealthy according to his means, and the poor according to his means; A gift of a reasonable amount is due from those who wish to do the right things. (2:236)

6. O mankind! reverence your Guardian Lord, Who created you from a single Person, created, of like nature, his mate, and from them twain scattered (like seeds) countless men and women; Reverence Allah, through Whom ye demand your mutual (rights), and (reverence) the wombs (that bore you); for Allah ever watches over you. (4:1)

7. And give the women (on marriage) their dower as a free gift; but if they, of their own good pleasure, remit any part of it to you, take it and enjoy it with right good cheer. (4:4)

8. In what your wives leave, your share is a half, if they leave no child; but, if they leave a child, ye get a fourth; after payment of legacies and debts. In what ye leave, their share is a fourth, if ye leave no child. But if ye leave a child, they get an eighth; after payment of legacies and debts. (4:12)

9. O ye who believe! Ye are forbidden to inherit women against their will. Nor should ye treat them with harshness that ye may take away part of the dower ye have given them, except where they have been guilty of open lewdness; on the contrary live with them on a footing of kindness and equity. If ye take a dislike to them it may be that ye dislike a thing, and Allah brings about through it a great deal of good. (4:19)

10. But if ye decide to take one wife in place of another, even if ye had given the latter a whole treasure for dower, take not the least bit of it back: Would ye take it by slander and a manifest wrong? (4:20)

11. Men are the protectors and maintainers of women, because Allah has given the one more (strength) than the other, and because they support them from their means. Therefore the righteous women are devoutly obedient, and guard in (the husband's) absence what Allah would have them guard. As to those women on whose part ye fear disloyalty and ill conduct, admonish them (first) (next), refuse to share their beds, (and last) beat them (lightly); but if they return to obedience, seek not against them means (of annoyance):Foy Allah is Most High, great (above you all). (4:34)

12. If ye fear a breach between them twain, appoint (two) arbiters, one from his family, and the other from hers; if they wish for peace, Allah will cause, their reconciliation: for Allah hath full knowledge, and is acquainted with all things. (4:35)

13. It is He Who created you from a single person, and made his mate of like nature, in order that he might dwell with her (in love). When they are united, she bears a light burden and carries it about (unnoticed). When she grows heavy, they both pray to Allah their Lord, (saying); "If Thou gives us a goodly child, we vow we shall (ever) be grateful." (7:189)

14. And Allah has made for you mates (and companions) of your own nature, and made for you, out of them, sons and daughters and grandchildren, and provided for you sustenance of the best: will they then believe in vain things, and be ungrateful for Allah's favours. (16:72)

15. And among His Signs is this that He created for you mates from among yourselves, that ye may dwell in tranquillity with them, and He has put love and mercy between your (hearts): Verily in that are Signs for those who reflect. (30:21)

16. Let the women live (in 'iddat), in the same style as ye live, according to your means: Annoy them not, so as to restrict them. And if they carry (life in their wombs), then spend (your substance) on them until they deliver their burden: and if they suckle your (offspring), give them

their recompense: and take mutual counsel together, according to what is just and reasonable. And if ye find yourselves in difficulties, let another woman suckle (the child) on the (father's) behalf. (65:6)

Ahadith of Hadrat Muhammad (may Allah's peace be on him) on the rights of the wives are:

1. Abu Omamah reported from the Messenger of Allah who used to say: Next to fear of Allah the believer finds nothing good for him than a virtuous wife. If he bids her, she obeys him; if he looks at her she gives him pleasure; if he gives her a promise, she fulfils it, and if he is absent from her, she guards herself and his property. (Ibn Majah)

2. Abu Hurairah reported from the Holy Prophet who said: When a man has two wives and he does not deal equitably between them, he will come on the Resurrection Day with a side hanging down. (Tirmizi, Abu Daud, Nisai)

3. Hakim b Muawiyah from his father reported: I asked: O Messenger of Allah! What right has the wife of one among us got over him? He said it is that you shall give her food when you have taken your food, that you shall clothe her when you have clothed yourself, that you shall not slap her on the face, nor revile (her), nor leave (her) alone except within the house. (Ahmad, Abu Daud, Ibn Majah)

4. Abu Hurairah reported that the Messenger of Allah said: The most perfect of the believers in faith is he who is the best of them in conduct, and the best of you are those who are the best to their wives. [Tirmizi (approved, correct)]

5. Aber b Abdullah reported that the Messenger of Allah said: Fear Allah regarding women. Verily you have married them with trust of Allah and made their private parts lawful with the word of Allah. You have got (rights) over them that they entertain nobody to your beds which you dislike. If they do this, give them a beating without causing injury. They have got (rights) over you in respect of their food and clothing according to means. (Bukhari and Muslim)

6. Anas reported that the Messenger of Allah said: When a woman says her five (prayers) and fasts her month, and guards her private parts, and obeys her husband, let her enter Paradise by whichever door she likes. (Abu Nayeem in Hilya)

7. Abu Hurairah reported that a man came to the Messenger of Allah and said: I have got a dinar. He said: Spend it for yourself. He said: I have got another. He said: Spend it for your children. He said: I have got another, He said: Spend it for your wife. He said: I have got another. He replied: Spend it for your servant: He said: I have got another. He replied: you know best. (Abu Daud, Nisai)

8. Abu Hurairah reported that the Messenger of Allah said: (As for) a dinar you have spent in the way of Allah, and a dinar you have spent in emancipating a slave, and a dinar you have given to a poor man in charity and a dinar you have spent for your family, the greatest of them in reward is that which you have spent for your family. (Muslim)

9. Abu Hurairah reported that the Messenger of Allah said: Let no believing man hate a believing woman. If he hates one trait of her character, he shall be pleased with another that is within her. (Muslim)

10. Nothing among the choicest blessings of this world is better than a virtuous wife. (Ibn Majah)

11. It is reported by Abdullah bin Umar that during the life time of the Holy Prophet, the companions treated their wives most politely for fear that a Commandment concerning them might be revealed, and not until he had passed away did they begin talking with them freely." (Bukhari)

(Dr. Muhammad Sharif Chaudhry was born in a devout religious family of farmers at village Gareywala in Kasur District of the Punjab, Pakistan on November 5, 1944. In 2000, at fairly advanced age of 56 he has obtained Ph.D. in Comparative Religion from U.S.A. He enjoys an extremely brilliant academic career with first divisions, scholarships, and merit positions).

There is no compulsion in religion according to the Quran: "There is no compulsion in religion. Verily, the Right Path has become distinct from the wrong path. Whoever disbelieves in Taghut [anything worshipped other then the Real God (Allah)] and believes in Allah, then he has grasped the most trustworthy handhold that will never break. And Allah is All-Hearer, All-Knower." (Al-Baqarah 2:256).

Muslim women are not forbidden from going out in the community, working, or visiting relatives and female friends.

Allah (J) instructed the wife's of the Prophet (S) in these words: "O wives of the Prophet! You are not like any other women. If you keep your duty (to Allah), then be not soft in speech, lest he is whose heart is a disease (of hypocrisy or evil desire for adultery, etc.) should be moved with desire, but speak in an honourable manner. And stay in your houses, and do not display yourselves like that of the times of ignorance, and offer prayers perfectly (Iqamat-as-Salat), and give Zakat and obey Allah and His Messenger. Allah wishes only to remove Ar-Rijs (evil deeds and sins, etc.) from you, O members of the family [of the Prophet (SAW)], and to purify you with a thorough purification." (Chapter, Al-Ahzab 33:32-33)

Since the fall of the Taliban regime in 2001 women gradually begun to work their way back towards being contributors to the economy. In the last decade a large number of women became members of the National Assembly of Afghanistan (Afghan Parliament), such as Shukria Barakzai, Fauzia Gailani, Nilofar Ibrahimi, Fauzia Kofi, Malalai Joya, and Shinki Karookhel. Women Ministers, are Suhaila Seddiqi,Sima Samar, Husn Banu Ghazanfar, and Soraya Dalil. Habiba Sarabi, who belongs to the minority Hazara group, became the first female governor in Afghanistan.

The Final Human Rights Declaration of Hazrat Muhammad(S):

After praising, Allah, Hazrat Muhammad (S) declared: "O People, lend me an attentive ear, for I know not whether after this year, I shall ever be amongst you again. Therefore, listen to what I am saying to you very carefully and take these words to those who could not be present here today.

O People, just as you regard this month, this day, this city as Sacred, so regard the life and property of every Muslim as a sacred trust. Return the goods entrusted to you to their rightful owners. Hurt no one so that no one may hurt you. Remember that you will indeed meet your Lord, and that He will indeed reckon your deeds. God has forbidden you to take usury (interest), therefore all interest obligation shall henceforth be waived. Your capital, however, is yours to keep. You will neither inflict nor suffer any inequity. God has Judged that there shall

94

be no interest, and that all the interest due to Abbas ibn Abd'al Muttalib shall henceforth be waived...

Beware of Satan, for the safety of your religion. He has lost all hope that he will ever be able to lead you astray in big things, so beware of following him in small things.

O People, it is true that you have certain rights with regard to your women, but they also have rights over you. Remember that you have taken them as your wives only under a trust from God and with His permission. If they abide by your right then to them belongs the right to be fed and clothed in kindness. Do treat your women well and be kind to them for they are your partners and committed helpers. And it is your right that they do not make friends with any one of whom you do not approve, as well as never to be unchaste.

O People, listen to me in earnest, worship God, perform your five daily prayers, fast during the month of Ramadan, and offer Zakat. Perform Hajj if you have the means.

All mankind is from Adam and Eve. An Arab has no superiority over a non-Arab, nor does a non-Arab have any superiority over an Arab; white has no superiority over black, nor does a black have any superiority over white; [none have superiority over another] except by piety and good action. Learn that every Muslim is a brother to every Muslim and that the Muslims constitute one brotherhood. Nothing shall be legitimate to a Muslim which belongs to a fellow Muslim unless it was given freely and willingly. Do not, therefore, do injustice to yourselves.

Remember, one day you will appear before God and answer for your deeds. So beware, do not stray from the path of righteousness after I am gone.

O People, no prophet or apostle will come after me, and no new faith will be born. Reason well, therefore, O people, and understand words which I convey to you. I leave behind me two things, the Quran and my example, the Sunnah, and if you follow these you will never go astray.

All those who listen to me shall pass on my words to others and those to others again; and it may be that the last ones understand my words better than those who listen to me directly. Be my witness, O God, that I have conveyed your message to your people."

Appendix-1

THE AFGHAN TRANSIT TRADE AGREEMENT

[Kabul, the 2nd, March, 1965]

AGREEMENT BETWEEN THE GOVERNMENT OF THE ISLAMIC REPUBLIC OF PAKISTAN AND THE GOVERNMENT OF THE KINGDOM OF AFGHANISTAN FOR REGULATION OF TRAFFIC IN TRANSIT

The Government of the Islamic Republic of Pakistan and the Government of the Kingdom of Afghanistan being desirous of strengthening basis, improving the difficulties in the movement of goods through the two countries, and having taken into consideration the present volume and future development of transit trade, have decided to conclude an agreement and to this and have appointed their plenipotentiaries as under:--

The Government of the Islamic Republic of Pakistan, Wahiduzzaman, Minister for Commerce The Government of the Kingdom of Afghanistan, Mohammad Sarwar Omar, Minister for Commerce Who have exchanged their full powers, found in good and due form, have agreed to the following articles:--

Article-I

The Contracting Parties undertake in accordance with the provisions of this Agreement to grant and guarantee to each other the freedom of transit to and from their territories.

No distinction shall be made which is based on the flag of vessels, the place of origin, departure, entry, exit or destination or any other circumstances relating to the ownership of goods, of vessels or of other means of transport.

Article-II

Goods including baggage, and vessels and other means of transport shall be deemed to be in transit across the territory of a Contracting Party, when the passage across such territory or without transhipment, warehousing, breaking bulk or change in the mode of transport, is only a portion of a complete journey beginning and terminating beyond the frontier of the contracted parties across whose territory the traffic passes – Traffic of this nature in this Agreement 'Traffic in Transit.'

Article-III

The transit routes shall be:

(1)-Peshawar – Torkham and vice versa.

(2)-Chaman – Spin Boldak and vice versa.

Additional routes may be agreed between the Contracting Parties from time to time. Goods moving via these routes shall be entered at the proper Customs post prescribed by each Party. Adequate transit and other facilities shall be provided by the Contracting Party concerned at these posts.

Article—IV

No Customs duties, taxes, dues, or charges of any kind whether national, provincial or municipal regardless of their name and purposes, shall be levied on traffic in transit except charges for transportation or those commensurate with the administrative expenses entailed by traffic in transit or with the cost of services rendered.

With a view to achieving simplification of existing Customs Practices and Procedures, the contracting Parties agree to adopt at points of entry and exit the procedures laid down in the Annex to this Agreement.

Article—V

Without prejudice to the generality of the provisions contained in Article III, the Government of the Islamic Republic of Pakistan shall earmark sheds and open spaces in the Karachi Port Area, to be known as Afghan Transit Area, for the good sin transit to and from Afghanistan. For Hazardous and awkward goods separate arrangements for storage will be made indicated in the Annex.

Article—VI

The two Contracting Parties recognising the importance of the Kabul-Torkham-Peshawar transit route have decided to examine all matters pertinent to the development of this route, including further consideration of the extension of the railway from Landi Khana to Torkham.

Article—VII

The Government of the Islamic Republic of Pakistan undertake to meet in full, the requirements of wagons for transit traffic on both Karachi-Spin Boldak and Peshwar-Karachi routes.

Article—VIII

Each Contracting shall appoint Liaison Officers to look into the working of this Agreement, and to refer, for expeditious solution, to the appropriate authorities of their own country and to the Liaison Officer of the other country, any question arising from the operation of this Agreement. The Liaison Officers will meet as often as necessary and in any case not less than once in six months and the contracting Parties shall provide them with the necessary facilities.

Article—IX

The Contracting Parties agree that railway freight, port and other dues shall be subject to the most sympathetic consideration and shall be no less favourable than those imposed by either Party on goods owned by its own nationals.

Article—X

Nothing in this Agreement shall be construed to prevent the adoption and enforcement by either Party of measures necessary to protect public morals, human, animal or plant life or health and for the security of its own territory.

Article—XI

The Contracting Parties shall meet and consult each other once a year to review the working of this Agreement.

Article—XII

The Contracting Parties agree to resolve any difference relating to the misinterpretation of this Agreement by negotiation, and in the even of failure to reach a settlement, to refer the matter to an arbitrator acceptable to both Parties, whose decision shall be binding.

Article—XIII

Nothing in this Agreement or its Annexes will affect in any way the political stand of the two countries or the political difference existing between them, and the contracting Parties fully reserve their rights with regard to these subjects.

Article—XIV

This Agreement shall be ratified and the Instruments of Ratification shall be exchanged at Rawalpindi. The Agreement shall come into force from the date of the exchange of the Instruments of Ratification and shall remain in force for five years from the date it comes into force. Unless notice of termination is given in writing by either Contracting Party to the other six months before the expiration of the five years period, the Agreement shall be automatically renewed for a further period of five years. It can be thereafter be terminated by either Party at any time provided six months notice of termination is given by either party.

Article—XV

The present Agreement is drawn in duplicate in English and Dari Languages, both texts being equally valid.

IN WITNESS THEREFORE, the undersigned, being duly authorised by their respective Governments, have signed, the present Agreement. Done in duplicate in English and Dari at Kabul on 2nd March, 1965.For the Government of the Islamic For the Government of Republic of Pakistan. The Kingdom of Afghanistan.

Sd/-   Sd/-

WAHIDUZZAMAN MOHAMMAD. MINISTER FOR COMMERCE. SARWAR OMAR, MINISTER FOR COMMERCE.

PROTOCOL ANNEXED TO TRANSIT AGREEMENT SIGNED BETWEEN THE GOVERNMENT OF THE ISLAMIC REPUBLIC OF PAKISTAN AND THE GOVERNMENT OF THE KINGDOM OF AFGHANISTAN DATED MARCH 2, 1965

In accordance with the provisions of the Agreement signed in Kabul between the authorised representatives of the Contracting Parties on March 2, 1965, regulating Traffic in Transit to and from Afghanistan, the signatories, in order to regulate the transport of goods by lorries from Peshawar to Kabul, and from Chaman to Kandahar and vice versa until such a time as extension of rail and road is completed, have agreed as follows:

Article—I

The two Governments agree that there shall be open competition for all transporters for carriage of all categories of goods to and from Afghanistan irrespective of ownership of goods.

Article—2

The two Governments agree to accord to transporters and clearing and forwarding agents from either country national treatment.

Article—3

Determination of freight rates shall be left to market conditions for goods of all descriptions and denominations. No discrimination shall be made by the authorities of either Government in the matter of allocation of freight as between the transporters of either country.

Article—4

Each Government agrees that no taxes shall be levied by it on transport vehicles registered in the territory of the other country except by prior consultation and on basis of equality.

Article—5

The two Governments agree that (a) Route permits shall be issued by the country in which the vehicles are registered; (b) Driving Licenses and certificates of fitness in respect of transport vehicles covered by this Protocol issued in one country shall be valid in the other country also. Vehicles carrying petroleum and petroleum products shall continue to be governed by existing practice regarding certificates of fitness; and

(c) The period for which vehicles of one country of may stay in the other on each trip shall be fixed on uniform reciprocal basis.

Article—6

The two Governments agree to grant to transporters multiple entry visas valid for a period of six months at a time.

Article—7

The two Governments agree to grant to transport vehicles road permits for a period of six months at a time.

Article—8

The two Governments shall consult each other with a view to adopting necessary measures to facilitate the flow of traffic between the two countries and shall seek all possible means within their power to remove any factors which may damage the normal accomplishment of the operation foreseen in this Protocol.

Article—9

This Protocol shall come into force simultaneously with the Agreement on Traffic in Transit signed on 2nd, March, 1965.

Done in duplicate in English and Dari both texts equally authentic, in Kabul on the 2nd, March, 1965.

Signed on behalf of the Signed on behalf of the Government of the Government of the Islamic Republic of Pakistan. Kingdom of Afghanistan.

WAHIDUZZAMAN, MOHAMMAD MINISTER FOR COMMERCE.

SARWAR OMAR, MINISTER FOR COMMERCE

ANNEX ON THE CUSTOMS AND OTHER PROCEDURES TO THE AGREEMENT SIGNED ON THE 2 ND MARCH, 1965 BETWEEN THE GOVERNMENT OF THE ISLAMIC REPUBLIC OF PAKISTAN AND THE ROYAL AFGHAN GOVERNMENT FOR REGULATING TRAFFIC IN TRANSIT.

1. CUSTOMS AND OTHER PROCEDURES IN RESPECT OF GOODS AND PASSENGER'S UNACCOMPANIED BAGGAGE ENTERING PAKISTAN FOR TANSIT TO AFGHANISTAN.

1. On arrival of the goods the owner or his agent shall at the time of entering them at the Custom House.

(a) Declare that the goods are intended for such transit;

(b) Furnish in quadruplicate an invoice of the goods so declared in the prescribed form specifying herein f by which the two authorised routes the goods are intended to be transported viz.

(i)-Peshawar—Torkham

(ii)-Chaman—Spin Boldak

(c)-On compliance with the above provisions the documents will be completed on the basis of exemption from duty, Sales-tax and import trade control regulations after such inspection as may be considered necessary.

2. The further procedure in respect of goods arriving through Karachi will be as follows:

The goods will be sealed with Customs seal and removed from the Karachi Port Trust transit sheds, under Customs supervision, to the Afghan transit sheds specially set apart for the purpose under Customs physical control. Heavy goods such as machinery and iron or steel, etc. will be removed from the Karachi Port Trust transit areas under customs supervision and stored in enclosed open spaces, specially provided for the purpose, under Customs control.

Explosives and hazardous goods and heavy cargo exceeding 5 tons in weight for which special storage arrangements have been provided by the Karachi Port Trust will not be removed to the transit shed or open space set apart for Afghan Transit goods.

3.The goods will be loaded under Customs supervision into railway wagons, exclusively provided for in-transit goods, which will be sealed by the Railway. In the case of open wagons loading heavy articles such as cars, trucks, machinery, iron and steel, etc. sealing may be dispensed with the original copy of the invoice duty checked and completed by the Customs will be handed over to the owner or his agent. At the same time the duplicate and triplicate copies of the invoice will be dispatched by the Custom House to the Afghan Customs at Spin Boldak.

4. On receipt of the invoice from the Pakistan Customs, the Afghan Customs at Spin Boldak will retain the duplicate and return the triplicate copy to the Custom House of despatch in Pakistan with appropriate endorsement certifying the arrival of the goods.

5. The procedure in respect of goods despatched by the Peshawar and Torkham route from Karachi will be the same as detailed up to and including paragraph 3 above in respect of Spin Boldak. The procedure thereafter will be that the Custom House will despatch the duplicate and triplicate copies of the invoices to the Customs Officer at Peshawar. On receipt of the invoice from the Karachi Customs, the Customs Officer at Peshawar will retain the duplicate and forward the triplicate copy to the Customs Officer at Torkham.

On arrival at Peshawar such goods will be carried to a transit shed or area under Customs control or transferred directly to a road transport under Customs supervision. Road transports in which the goods are carried forward to Afghanistan will, where possible, be sealed with Customs Seal.

6. Goods which require re-packing after arrival at Peshawar will be allowed re-packing facilities at the Transit shed or area under Customs control. The Customs Officer at Peshawar will check the goods with the original copy of the invoice and compare the latter with the duplicate copy received from the port of entry.

If the seals are intact and the goods correspond with the description in the invoice, the Customs Officer shall allow the goods to be repacked and resealed under his supervision, shall endorse on each copy of the invoice details of any change in the number or description of the packages involved by such re-packing, shall where possible seal the road transport to Afghanistan return the original copy of the invoice so endorsed to the owner or his agent and forward the duplicate copy to Customs Officer at Torkham.

On arrival at Torkham, the goods must be presented to the Customs Officer along with the duplicate copy of the invoice for inspection and final clearance. The Customs Officer shall note the re-packing particulars, if any, on the reverse of the triplicate copy and return the duplicate to the Customs Officer at Peshawar.

7. In case of goods entering Pakistan at Lahore the procedure will be the same as detailed above in respect of Karachi except the provisions of paragraph 2 above.

8. The procedure in respect of goods moving into Spin Boldak will be enforced only when the railway line has been extended up to that point. Until then the formalities provided for in respect of Peshawar-Torkham route will apply mutatis mutandis to Chaman and to the Customs Post opposite Vesh.

9. Goods or passengers' unaccompanied baggage arriving in transit by sea at Karachi if moving by air to Afghanistan from Karachi airport will be transported under Customs seal to Karachi Airport and placed on board the on-carrying aircraft under Customs

supervision. The documentation in respect of such goods will be similar to that for goods despatched by rail with appropriate modifications.

II. PROCEDURE IN RESPECT OF GOODS AND PASSENGERS, UNACCOMPANIED BAGGAG MOVING IN TRANSIT FROM AFGHANISTAN TO FOREIGN COUNTRIES THROUGH PAKISTAN.

1. On entry of the goods at the land Customs stations at Torkham/Peshawar or at Chaman until such a time as the railway line is extended up to Spin Boldak and Torkham, the Afghan exporter or his agent shall declare that the goods are in transit to a third country or overseas and furnish in quadruplicate an invoice in the prescribed form.

2. The Government of Pakistan may require certain specified goods despatched in transit from Afghanistan to foreign countries to be sealed by the Afghan Customs before their despatch out of Afghanistan. A list of such goods will be furnished to the Government of Afghanistan from time to time.

3. On compliance with the above provisions the seals on the goods will be checked and the goods removed under Customs provisions to the transit shed or area at the Pakistan railhead at Peshawar or Chaman under Customs control. Re-packing facilities will be allowed at these transit sheds or areas as well as at the transit shed in the Karachi Port area.

4. The goods will be loaded under the Customs supervision into railway wagons exclusively provided for in-transit goods which will be sealed by the Railway.

The original copy of the invoice duly checked and completed by the Customs will be handed over to the owner or his agent. At the same time, the duplicate and triplicate copies of the invoice will be forwarded by the Frontier Customs Officer at the Pakistan railhead to the Collector of Customs, Karachi if the goods are to be exported by sea or to the Land Customs Officer at the Land Customs Station through which the goods are to be exported by land to India.

The quadruplicate copy will be retained by the Frontier Land Customs Officer for his record. The Customs Officer, who supervises the loading of goods into the railway wagons, will record on all copies of the invoice the numbers of the wagons in which the goods have been despatched.

(a) In the case of goods to be exported by sea from the Port of Karachi, the goods will, on arrival at Karachi railway station be unloaded from the wagons under Customs supervision after verifying that the seals are intact. They will then be carried under Customs supervision to the Afghan transit shed specially set apart for the purpose in the port area, under Customs control. The goods will remain in Customs control until they are duly exported on filing of an export shipping bill.

The goods will be inspected, and examined if necessary, before shipment is allowed under Customs supervision.

NOTE: Goods of hazardous nature such as cotton which are in transit from Afghanistan to foreign countries cannot be stored in the transit shed along with other goods and the present arrangements of storing such goods will continue.

(b) In the case of goods to be exported by Land to India, the wagons will, on arrival at the Land Customs Station, be inspected by the Customs. Detailed examination of the goods will be dispensed with if the seals on the wagons are intact.

5-The Customs Officer will satisfy himself that the seals are intact and that the numbers of the wagons correspond with those entered in the invoice. If the duplicate and triplicate copies of the invoice have not been received from the Frontier Customs Officer he will not detain the goods but will pass them after entering the verified particulars of the wagons and if necessary of the goods owner or his agent.

On receipt of the duplicate and triplicate copies of the invoice, he will make the necessary endorsement on the basis of the particulars recorded in his register.

6. After the goods have been duly shipped for export by sea or handed over to the railway authorities for onward transmission by land, the Customs Officer will certify on each copy of the invoice that the goods have been duly shipped or exported.

The original copy of the invoice will be returned to the owner or his agent, the duplicate copy will be sent to the Frontier Customs Officer at Peshawar or Chaman, as the case may be, and the triplicate copy will be retained for record by the Custom House, Karachi, or the Land Customs Station of export, as the case may be.

7. As soon as the Railway line is extended to Spin Boldak and Torkham the documentation and sealing of packages in respect of such goods will be the responsibility of the Afghan Customs, the sealing of wagons being done by the Railway, the detailed procedures respecting which will be drawn up by mutual consultation by representatives of the two Governments.

Appendix-2

Islamic Republic of Afghanistan

Counter Narcotics Drug Law, 17 December 2005

English translation prepared from the Official Dari, By Dr. Abdul Jabbar Sabit, Legal Advisor to the Ministry of Interior.

CHAPTER I

General Provisions

Article 1:

Basis

This Law is enacted pursuant to Article 7 of the Constitution of Afghanistan in order to prevent the cultivation of opium poppy, cannabis plants, and coca bush, and the trafficking of narcotic drugs, and to control psychotropic substances, chemical precursors, and equipment used in manufacturing, producing, or processing of narcotic drugs and psychotropic substances.

Article 2:

Objectives

The objectives of this Law are:

1. To prevent the cultivation of opium poppy, cannabis plants, and coca bush, and prescribe penalties for persons engaging in these activities.

2. To regulate and control narcotic drugs, psychotropic substances, chemical precursors, and substances and equipment used in the manufacture, production, or processing of narcotic drugs and psychotropic substances in order to prevent their use for illicit purposes and to ensure their use for medical, scientific, research and industrial purposes in accordance with the provisions of the law.

3. To prescribe penalties for persons engaging in and to prevent the cultivation, production, processing, acquisition, possession, distribution, manufacture, trade, brokering, importation, exportation, transportation, offering, use, storage, and concealment of narcotic drugs and psychotropic substances, and of the chemical precursors, other illicit substances, and equipment used for these illicit activities.

4. To coordinate, monitor, and evaluate the counter narcotics activities, policies, and programs of the Government of the Islamic Republic of Afghanistan.

5. To encourage farmers to cultivate licit crops instead of opium poppy, coca bush, and cannabis plants.

6. To establish health centers for detoxification, treatment, rehabilitation, and harm reduction services for drug-addicted and drug dependent persons in order to reintegrate them into society.

7. To attract the cooperation and assistance of national and international organizations in the task of combating cultivation, trafficking and use of narcotic drugs, psychotropic substances, and the chemical precursors used in their production, manufacturing, and processing.[4]

ARTICLE 3:

Definitions

Terms: The following terms have the following meanings in this law:

1) "Narcotic Drug" means a plant, substance or preparation classified as such in the

Tables annexed to this law.

2) "Analogue" means any substance which is not included in any of the Tables annexed to this law but whose chemical structure combination and whose psychotropic effects are similar to those of a substance included in the Tables annexed to this law

3) "Controlled delivery" means allowing the transportation and passage of illicit or suspected consignments of prohibited articles, including drugs, precursors, analogues or substances substituted for them, equipment of clandestine laboratories, or laundered money into or through Afghanistan or one or more countries, with the knowledge and under the supervision of the competent law enforcement authorities, in efforts to identify persons and investigate and establish proof of criminal offenses.

4) "Dependence" is a condition in which the use of drugs is compulsive, and stopping gives rise to psychological and even physical disorders, which leads the person to continue using the drug.

5) "Detoxification treatment" means treatment intended to eliminate physical dependence on a drug.

6) "Drug abuse" and "illicit drug use" mean the use of any regulated drug without a medical prescription and medical instructions for non-scientific and non-medical purposes.

7) "Drug addict" means a person in a state of physical and/or psychic dependence on a drug.

8) "Industrial use" of a drug means its exclusive use in a manufacturing process.

9) "Medical prescription" means a written document signed by a physician or a person holding a medical license, issued for the medical treatment of a patient and authorizing the dispensing by a pharmacist to that person of a specific quantity of controlled drugs.

10) "Medical use" means the consumption or use of drugs controlled by this law under a medical prescription and in accordance with international conventions.

11) "Money-laundering" means the same concepts as defined under article 3 of the Law against Money-Laundering and Criminal Proceeds published in the Official Gazette No. 840 on 10.08.1383.

12) "Precursor" means a substance used in drug manufacture or processing and classified as such under Table IV of this law.

13) "Psychotropic substance" means a drug in one of the Tables annexed to the 1971 Convention on Psychotropic Substances.

14) "Regulated drugs" are defined as all plants and substances, including their chemical preparations and their derivatives, and chemical precursors that are listed in Tables 1 - 4, derived from the United Nations International Conventions on Drugs, attached to this law.

15) "Mixture" or "Compound" means any preparation that contains any detectable amount of a controlled or regulated drug substance under this law.

16) "Covert Operations" means the investigation of criminal offences by law enforcement agencies' use of methods that include surveillance, the use of informants, undercover operations and the exchange of intelligence with appropriate law enforcement agencies or other organisations.

17) "Vehicle" means any mode of transportation used in drug-trafficking].

18) "Undercover Operations" means operations carried out in secret by the police in which the officers' identities are concealed from third parties by the use of an alias and false identity so as to enable the infiltration of existing criminal groups in order to arrest suspected criminals.

19) "Surveillance" means the covert watching of a person or group of persons or the covert listening to their conversations over a period of time by a human being or through the use of technical devices.

20) "Secret or Electronic Surveillance" means surveillance authorized by a competent court in accordance with the provisions of law. This surveillance includes the following activities:

· watching in private places using human or technical means;

· interception of communications;

· opening of mail; and,

· inspection of bank accounts and records of other financial activity.

21) "Conspiracy" or "Complicity" means the same as defined under article 49 of the 1355

Penal Code published in the Official Gazette No. 347.

22) "Possession" means the ability to exert control over an object, including cases where a person is not in physical contact with the object, but has the power to exercise control over it, either directly or through others.

23) "Distribution" is the transfer or attempted transfer of possession from one person to another.

24) "Aid" or "abet" means the same as defined under article 39 of the 1355 Penal Code published in the Official Gazette No. 347.

25) "Attempt" means the same as defined under article 29 of the 1355 Penal Code published in the Official Gazette No. 347.

26) "Public official" shall mean any officer, employee, or person acting for, on behalf, or under the authority of a government agency.

27) "Official act" shall mean any decision or action on any matter, controversy, or legal proceeding by a public official.

28) "Bribe" shall mean corruptly giving, offering, or promising anything of value to any person or entity, directly or indirectly, with the purpose of:

(1) influencing an official act;

(2) influencing a public official to commit or omit any act in violation of his

lawful duty; or

(3) influencing witnesses, detection, investigation, or trial proceedings;

(4) compelling any witness to be absent from any legal or court proceedings;

(5) influencing any agency, commission, or officer authorized by the law to hear and record the testimony of witnesses. 29) "Weapon" means any beating or injuring tools and devices, firearms, and explosives capable of inflicting injury or destruction, or that can cause death.

CHAPTER II

Classification and regulation of narcotic drugs, psychotropic substances, and chemicals used in the manufacture, production, or processing of narcotic drugs and psychotropic substances

Article 4:

Classification and Regulation of Narcotic Drugs

1. For purposes of this law, regulated drugs are defined as all plants and substances that are listed in Tables 1-3, including their chemical derivatives, and all chemical precursors that are listed in Table 4 of the Tables attached hereto. The regulated drugs covered by this law shall be classified in four tables:

• Table 1: Prohibited plants and substances with no medical use;

• Table 2: Strictly controlled plants and substances with a medical use;

• Table 3: Controlled plants and substances with a medical use;

• Table 4: Chemical precursors and other substances used in the illicit manufacture or processing of narcotic drugs and psychotropic substances.

Article 5:

Drug Regulation Committee

1) A Drug Regulation Committee is hereby established which shall be composed of five members with the following composition:

a) One medical and one pharmaceutical expert from the Ministry of Public Health;

b) Two experts from the Ministry of Counter-Narcotics;

c) One customs expert from the Ministry of Finance.

2) Members of the Drug Regulation Committee mentioned in paragraph 1 of this Article shall be appointed by their respective ministries for a period of four years. The Chairperson of the Drug Regulation Committee shall be appointed by the Minister of Counter-Narcotics from among its members.

3) Decisions and regulations of the Drug Regulation Committee shall be made by a majority of its members and shall be recorded in a special book.

4) In case any member of the Drug Regulation Committee fails to carry out his/her duties in a satisfactory fashion, he/she can be removed from his membership in the Committee by the Minister of Counter Narcotics.

5) The administrative costs of the Drug Regulation Committee and those of its secretariat shall be paid directly from the budget of the Ministry of Counter Narcotics.

Members of the Drug Regulation Committee shall be paid appropriate attendance fees by the Ministry of Counter-Narcotics.[8]

6) The Drug Regulation Committee shall prepare one quarterly and one annual report to the Minister of Counter Narcotics on its activities. The Minister may direct the Drug Regulation Committee to provide the necessary information in accordance with this Law and relevant regulations.

7) The Drug Regulation Committee will hereinafter be called the Committee.

Article 6:

Duties of the Committee

1. The classifications of the regulated drugs in Tables 1 through 4 shall be established and amended, in particular by new inclusions, deletions, or transfers from one Table to another, by the Committee, taking into account any amendments or additions ordered by the United Nations Commission on Narcotic Drugs. Plants and substances shall be included under their international non-proprietary name or, failing this, under their commercial, scientific, or common name.

2. The Committee may not include an internationally controlled substance in a Table subject to a regime less strict than that required under the United Nations Conventions for the substance in question.

3. The Committee shall not transfer any substance from Table 1 to Table 2 or 3, except as provided in paragraph 1 of this Article.

4. Inclusions, deletions or transfers from one Table to another in accordance with paragraphs 1, 2, and 3 above shall be valid when they are published in the official gazette.

5. Except as otherwise provided by this law, a preparation, compound, or mixture of any regulated drug shall be subject to the same regulations, prohibitions, and penalties as the regulated drug which it contains, and if it contains two or more regulated drugs it shall be subject to the conditions governing the most strictly controlled regulated drug that it contains.

6. A preparation, compound, or mixture containing a substance listed in Tables 2, 3 or 4 that is compounded in such a way as to present no, or a negligible, risk of abuse or diversion and from which the substance cannot be recovered by readily applicable means in a quantity liable to illicit use, abuse, or diversion may be exempt from certain of the control measures set forth in this law by decision of the Committee.

7. If the substances listed in Tables 2 and 3 and their preparations can be used in medicine they shall be subject to the provisions applicable to all substances and preparations intended for use in human or veterinary medicine to the extent that such provisions are compatible with those established in this law.[9]

CHAPTER III

Licensing, Cultivation, Production, Manufacture, Trade, Distribution, and Use of Plants, Substances and Preparations Listed in Tables 1, 2, 3, and 4

Article 7:

Licenses

1. No person shall cultivate, produce, process, manufacture, trade, distribute, possess, supply, traffic, transport, transfer, acquire, purchase, sell, import, export, or transit, plants, substances and preparations listed in Tables 2 and 3 in the territory of Afghanistan, unless he has been licensed by the Committee.

2. No person may engage in any of the operations set forth in paragraph 1 of this article at any building or on any premises not expressly identified on a license issued under this Article, or separately licensed by the Committee for use by specially designated State enterprises, or exempt from licensing under this law.

3. The Committee may issue a license to cultivate, manufacture, distribute(including dispensing), import or export one or more of the plants, substances and preparations listed in Tables 1, 2 and 3 at the building or on the premises identified in the license. Such a license shall permit any of the operations set for thin the first paragraph of this article that are necessarily involved in the licensed activity.

4. A license to engage in the operations set forth in paragraph 1 of this article may be issued only if the use of the plants, substances and preparations in question is restricted to medical or scientific purposes. This license shall be valid for one year. Licensing shall be subject to verification of the character and professional qualifications of the applicant. A license may not be granted to any person convicted of a narcotics or money laundering offense.

5. The industrial production and use of a substance listed in Tables 1, 2 or 3 for other than medical or scientific purposes may be authorized by the Committee if the applicant satisfactorily shows that such production or use is necessary to a industrial process, he shall ensure that the products manufactured, other than another regulated drug subject to this Law, cannot be abused or produce harmful effects, and he shall ensure that any regulated drug included in this authorization and used in the composition of the products manufactured cannot be easily recovered. The person or entity so authorized shall destroy all quantities of the regulated drug included in this authorization that cannot be rendered harmless or sufficiently irretrievable and reports to the Committee the quantity of the regulated drug produced, used or destroyed.[10]

6. A person can operate in places set forth in paragraphs 3 and 7 of this article which have been designated for the manufacture, distribution (including dispensing), importation or exportation of regulated drugs only when those places comply with the security standards established by the Committee.

7. State enterprises specially designated by the Committee to engage in the operations set forth in paragraph 1 of this article shall be required to apply for a license to use buildings and premises for such operations, and the Committee may issue such license in accordance with the requirements of paragraph 6 of this Article.

8. For the better implementation of this article, the Committee may establish regulations, in particular those governing applications for and the granting, content, scope, withdrawal and suspension of licenses.

Article 8:

Possessing Needed Amounts of Narcotic Drugs

1. Authorized regulated drug manufacturers and distributors may hold the quantities of the various regulated drugs required for the smooth functioning of business. The distributors who only dispense regulated drugs are accepted from this provision.

2. The Committee shall establish for each year, taking into account the prevailing market conditions, the anticipated medical, scientific, research, and industrial needs for the regulated drugs in Tables 1, 2 and 3, and the anticipated lawful exports of such regulated drugs, the maximum quantities of these regulated drugs that shall be manufactured and the maximum quantities that each licensee and each specially designated State enterprise shall be entitled to manufacture. These limits may be changed during the year if necessary.

3. The Committee may establish and publish regulations and procedures for the implementation of this Article.

Article 9:

Exports and imports

1. The export and import of substances on Tables 1, 2 and 3 shall be subject to separate authorization issued by the Committee.

2. This authorization shall be subject to the completion of a form which includes the requirements established by the Committee and the United Nations Economic and Social Council. [11]

3. The Committee may authorize an importation of a substance listed in Tables1, 2, or 3 only to meet legitimate medical, scientific, and industrial needs. The import authorization shall not be necessary in the event of a catastrophe or an emergency as determined by the Committee, but the importer shall maintain a record of the importation as prescribed by the Committee.

4. The Committee may authorize an exportation of a substance listed on Tables 1, 2, or 3 only to a country that maintains effective controls over the use of the regulated drug and

only if the regulated drug is to be used for medical, scientific, or other legitimate purposes.

5. An authorization for the importation or exportation of a substance listed on Tables 1, 2, or 3 is not transferable.

6. An application for import or export authorization of a substance listed on Tables 1, 2, or 3 shall indicate the following:

a) The name and address of the importer or exporter;

b) The names and addresses of any consignee, if known;

c) The international non-proprietary name of each substance or, failing this, the name of the substance in the tables of the international conventions;

d) The pharmaceutical form and characteristics of each substance and, in the case of a preparation, its trade name;

e) The quantity of each substance and preparation involved in the operation;

f) The period during which the operation is to take place;

g) The mode of transport or shipment; and

h) The border custom house of the importation and exportation.

7. An import certificate or other documentation issued by the Government of the importing country shall be attached to the export application.

8. An import or export authorization shall contain, in addition to the expiration date and the name of the issuing authority, the same types of details as the application.

9. The import authorization shall specify whether the import is to be effected in a single consignment or may be affected in more than one consignment, and shall establish the time in which the import of all consignments must be affected.

10. The export authorization shall also indicate the number and date of the import certificate issued by the Government of the importing country;

11. A copy of the export authorization shall accompany each consignment and the Committee shall send a copy to the Government of the importing country.

12. If the quantity of plants, substances or preparations actually exported is smaller than that specified in the export authorization, and is certified by the customs [12] office, the Committee shall note that fact on the related document and on all official copies thereof.

13. Once the consignment has entered the national territory or when the period stipulated in the import authorization has expired, the Committee shall send the export

authorization to the Government of the exporting country, with an endorsement specifying the quantity of each regulated drug actually imported.

14. Commercial documents such as invoices, cargo manifests, customs or transport documents and other shipping documents shall include the name of the plants and substances as set out in the tables of the international conventions and the trade name of the preparations, the quantities exported from the national territory or to be imported into it, and the names and addresses of the exporter, the importer and the consignee.

15. Exports from the national territory of consignments to the address or account of a person other than the person named in the import certificate issued by the Government of the importing country or in other documentation demonstrating authorization for the import into that country shall be prohibited. This same provision shall apply to the importation of consignments into the national territory.

16. Exports from the national territory of consignments to a bonded warehouse shall be prohibited unless the Government of the importing country certifies on the import certificate or other authorization that it has approved such a consignment. 17. Imports to the national territory of consignments to a bonded warehouse shall be prohibited unless the Government certifies on the import certificate that it approves such a consignment. Withdrawal from the bonded warehouse shall require a permit from the authorities having jurisdiction over the warehouse. In the case of a consignment to a foreign destination, such withdrawal shall be treated as if it were a new export within the meaning of the present Article.

The regulated drugs stored in the bonded warehouse may not be subjected to any process, which would modify their nature, nor may their packaging be altered without the permission of the authorities having jurisdiction over the warehouse.

18. A consignment entering or leaving the national territory which is not accompanied by a proper import or export authorization or does not comply with the authorization shall be detained by the competent authorities until the legitimacy of the consignment is established or until a court rules on its status.

19. The Committee shall specify those customs offices operating in the national territory that are to deal with the import or export of the regulated drugs listed in Tables 1, 2 and 3.

The transit of any consignment of plants, substances or preparations listed in Tables 1, 2 and 3 through the national territory shall be prohibited, whether or not the consignment is removed from the conveyance in which it is carried, unless a copy of the export authorization issued by the Government of the exporting country for such consignment is produced to the department designated by the Committee

21. The route specified by the export license for a consignment which is in transit in Afghanistan shall not be changed.

22. An application for authorization to change the itinerary or the consignee shall be treated as if the export in question were from the national territory to the new country or consignee concerned.

23. No consignment of plants, substances and preparations in transit through the national territory may be subjected to any process that might change their nature, nor may its packaging be altered without the permission of the Committee.

24. If there is a conflict between the provisions of this article and those of an international agreement that Afghanistan has signed, the provisions of the international agreement prevail.

25. The provisions of this article shall not apply where the consignment in question is transported by air to another country. If the aircraft stops over or makes an emergency landing in the national territory, the consignment shall be treated as an export from the national territory to the country of destination only if it is removed from the aircraft.

26. Free ports and free trade zones shall be subject to the same controls and supervision as other parts of the national territory regarding the importation of plants, substances, or preparations listed in Tables 1, 2 and 3.

27. Transport companies and enterprises shall abide by the regulations of the Committee with regard to taking reasonable measures to prevent the use of their means of transport for illicit trafficking in the regulated drugs covered by the present law, and shall also be required:

• To submit cargo manifests in advance, whenever possible;

• To keep the products in sealed containers having tamper-resistant, individually verifiable seals, and in which every kind of alteration should be easily discernable;

• To report to the appropriate authorities, at the earliest opportunity, any suspicious consignments.[14]

Article 10:

Retail Trade and Distribution

1. Purchases of regulated drugs listed in Tables 2 and 3 for the purpose of professional supply may be made only from a private individual or state enterprise holding a license issued under this law.

2. Only the following persons and state entities may, without having to apply for a license, purchase and hold plants and regulated drugs listed in Tables 2 and 3 for their professional needs:

• Pharmacists holding a license to practice when acting in the usual course of business as an agent or employee of a person or entity holding a valid license to distribute regulated drugs;

• Pharmacists at a public or private hospital or health care institutions that is licensed to distribute regulated drugs when acting in the usual course of business as an agent or employee of that hospital or health care institutions;

• Pharmacists holding a license to practice in charge of public or private warehouses;

• Hospitals or health care institutions without a pharmacist in charge, in emergency cases and unanticipated events provided that a qualified physician attached to the establishment who holds a license to practice and to dispense regulated drugs has agreed to take responsibility for the stocks in question;

• Physicians, dental surgeons, and veterinary surgeons holding a license to practice and authorized to dispense regulated drugs, including the preparations included in a list drawn up by the Committee;

3. Physicians, dental surgeons, and veterinary surgeons holding a license to practice may, without having to apply for a drug distribution license, purchase and hold the needed quantities of preparations included in a list drawn up by the Committee.

4. Dental surgeons, midwives, and nurses holding a license to practice may, without having to apply for a license, purchase and hold for their professional activities quantities of preparations included in a list drawn up by the Committee.

5. The regulated drugs listed in Tables 2 and 3 may be prescribed to individuals and animals only in the form of pharmaceutical preparations and only on a medical prescription issued by one of the following professionals:[15]

• A physician holding a license to practice and to dispense regulated drugs;

• A dental surgeon holding a license to practice and to dispense regulated drugs, for treatment of a dental nature;

• A veterinary surgeon holding a license to practice and to dispense regulated drugs, for treatment of animals;

• A nurse or midwife holding a license to practice for treatment connected with their professional duties and within the limits set by the competent authority.

6. Pharmaceutical preparations listed in Tables 2 and 3 may be dispensed only by:

• Dispensing pharmacists holding a license;

• Pharmacists at public or private hospitals or health care institutions when such hospitals or institutions hold a license to dispense regulated drugs;

• Physicians and veterinary surgeons holding a license to practice and authorized to dispense regulated drugs;

• Nurses and midwives in the conduct of their professional duties.

7. The Committee, if the situation so requires and under such conditions as it may determine, may authorize, in all or part of the national territory, licensed pharmacists or any other licensed retail distributors to supply, without prescription, small quantities of therapeutic doses of pharmaceutical preparations containing one or more of the regulated drugs listed in Table 3.

8. The Committee shall establish regulations for the implementation of this Article, in particular the rules concerning the writing and filling of prescriptions for pharmaceutical preparations listed in Tables 2 and 3.

Article 11:

Private institutions and state enterprises

1. Private institutions and State enterprises holding licenses to engage in operations involving regulated drugs shall furnish to the Committee in respect of their activities:

• Not later than 15 days after the end of each quarter, a quarterly report on the quantities of each substance and each preparation imported or exported, indicating the country of origin and the country of destination;[16]

• Not later than 5 May of each year, a report for the previous calendar year indicating:

o The quantities of each substance and each preparation produced or manufactured;

o The quantities of each substance used for producing preparations and other:

§ Other substances covered by the present legislation; and

0 Substances not covered by the present legislation;

0 The quantities of each substance and each preparation supplied for retail distribution, medical or scientific research or teaching;

o The quantities of each substance and each preparation in stock as of 29 March of the year to which the information refers;

o The quantities of each substance necessary for the new calendar year.

2. The Committee shall establish procedures for the purchase of and placing orders for plants, substances and preparations listed in Tables 2, 3, and 4 required for the conduct of professional activities.

3. The Committee shall establish procedures for any purchase, transfer, export, import or dispensing of plants, substances and preparations listed in Table 2, and all related

transactions shall be recorded in accordance with regulations established by the Committee.

4. Any person, private enterprise, or state enterprise holding, for professional purposes, any plants, substances and preparations listed in Tables 2, 3, and 4 shall be required to keep them under regulations established by the Committee so as to prevent theft or any other form of diversion.

5. Any person, private enterprise, State enterprise, medical or scientific institution engaged in any activity or operation involving plants, substances or preparations covered by the present law shall be controlled and monitored by regulations established by the Committee. Such control and monitoring shall extend to the compartments containing first-aid kits of public transport conveyances engaged in international travel. The Committee shall, in particular, arrange for inspectors or any other body legally empowered to conduct inspections to make ordinary inspections of the establishments, premises, stocks and records at least once every two years. Extraordinary inspections can be done at any time. [17]

Article 12:

Monitoring and Control

1. State enterprises, private enterprises, medical and scientific institutions and other persons referred to in Article 11 shall be required, at the beginning of each year, to make an inventory of the plants, substances and preparations listed in Tables 1, 2 and 3 held by them and to compare the total quantities in stock at the time of the previous inventory, calculated together with those entered over the previous year and the total quantities withdrawn during the year, with those held at the time of the latest inventory.

2. Licensees, pharmacists and persons authorized to dispense drugs through wholesale pharmacies or drugstores shall be required to make an inventory and calculate the balance as stipulated in paragraph 1 of this article.

3. Any discrepancies noted in a balance or between the results of the balance and those of the inventory shall be immediately reported by the licensee, pharmacist or person authorized to dispense drugs to the Committee, which shall acknowledge receipt of the notification.

4. It shall be forbidden to distribute substances and preparations listed in Tables 2 and 3 unless they are enclosed in wrappers or containers bearing their name and, in the case of consignments of substances and preparations listed in Table 2, a double red band.

5. The outer wrappings of parcels described in paragraph 4 shall bear no information other than the names and addresses of the sender and the consignee. They shall be sealed with the sender's mark.

6. The label under which a preparation is offered for sale shall indicate the names of the substances listed in Tables 1, 2 and 3 that it contains, together with their weight and percentage.

7. Labels accompanying packages for retail sale or distribution as described in paragraph 4 shall indicate the directions for use as well as the cautions and warnings necessary for the safety of the user.

8. If necessary, additional requirements in respect of packaging and labelling shall be stipulated by regulations established by the Committee.

Article 13:

Regulation of Substances (Precursors) In Table 4

1. The manufacture, distribution or trading of the substances listed in Table 4 shall be subject to the provisions of this article.[18]

2. Import or export authorizations shall be refused if a consignment is possibly [?!!!] intended for the illicit manufacture of narcotic drugs or psychotropic substances.

3. Export or import consignments of substances listed in Table 4 annexed to this law shall be clearly labelled to show their contents.

4. Any person who, because of his job requirements, becomes aware of the economic, industrial, trade or professional secrets or trade processes of the substances listed on Table 4 annexed to this law shall be required to avoid disclosing the same to other people.

5. Manufacturers, importers, exporters, wholesalers and retailers shall be required to enter in a register established by the Committee any purchase or transfer of substances listed in Table 4. The entry shall be made with no blank spaces, erasures or overwriting. It shall indicate the date of the transaction, the name and the quantity of the product purchased or transferred and the name, address and occupation of the purchaser and seller. However, retailers shall not be required to enter the name of the purchaser. The registers shall be kept for ten years pursuant to regulations established by the Committee.

6. Manufacturers, importers, exporters, wholesalers and retailers of the substances listed in Table 4 shall be required to inform the appropriate police authority of any orders or transactions that appear suspicious, in particular by reason of the quantity of the substances being purchased or ordered, the repetition of such orders or purchases or the means of payment or transport used.

7. If there is strong evidence to warrant the suspicion that a substance listed in Table 4 is for use in the illicit manufacture of a narcotic drug, such substance shall be immediately seized pending the outcome of a judicial investigation.

8. The Committee shall submit to the Minister of Counter-Narcotics information on the import and export of precursor substances listed in Table 4.

Article 14:

Medical and Scientific Research and Teaching

1. For purposes of medical or scientific research, teaching or forensic work, the Committee may authorize, in accordance with a separate procedure and without requiring the licenses referred to in this Chapter, the cultivation, manufacturing, acquiring, importation, use, or possession of plants, substances and preparations in Tables 1, 2 and 3 in quantities not exceeding those strictly necessary for the purpose in question.

2. The applicant of the authorization referred to in paragraph 1 of this article shall enter in a register, which he shall keep for 5 years, the quantities of plants,[19] substances and preparations that he imports, acquires, manufactures, uses, and destroys. He shall also record the dates of the operations and the names of his suppliers. He shall furnish the Committee with an annual report on the quantities used or destroyed and those held in stock. The Committee shall be entitled to inspect registers maintained in accordance with this provision.[20]

Chapter IV

Offenses and Penalties

Article 15:

Drug Trafficking Offenses and Penalties

1. Any person who engages in the following acts without a license or authorization issued according to the provisions of this law has committed a drug trafficking offense and shall be punished in accordance with the provisions of this law:

(a) The production, manufacture, distribution, possession, extraction, preparation, processing, offering for sale, purchasing, selling, delivery, brokerage, dispatch, transportation, importation, exportation, purchase, concealment, or storage of any substance or mixture containing a substance listed in Tables 1 through 3 annexed to this law;

(b) Any of the operations referred to in paragraph 1 of this article in relation to any chemicals or precursors listed in Table 4 for the illicit cultivation, production or manufacture of narcotic drugs or psychotropic substances.

Article 16:

Drug Trafficking Penalties

1. Whoever commits a drug trafficking offense involving the following quantities of heroin, morphine, or cocaine, or any mixture containing those substances, shall be sentenced as follows:

(i) Less than 10 grams, imprisonment for between 6 months and one year, and a fine of between 30,000 Afs and 50,000 Afs.

(ii) Between 10 grams and 100 grams, imprisonment for between one and three years, and a fine of between 50,000 and 100,000 Afs.

(iii) Between 100 grams and 500 grams, imprisonment for between three and five years, and a fine of between 100,000 Afs and 250,000 Afs.

(iv) Between 500g and 1kg, imprisonment for between seven and ten years, and a fine of between 300,000 Afs and 500,000 Afs.

(v) Between 1kg and 5kg, imprisonment for between ten and fifteen years, and a fine of between 500,000 Afs and 1,000,000Afs.

(vi) Over 5kg, life imprisonment, and a fine of between 1,000,000 Afs and 10,000,000Afs.[21]

2. Whoever commits a drug trafficking offense involving the following quantities of opium or any mixture containing that substance shall be sentenced as follows:

(i) Less than 10 grams, imprisonment for up to three months, and a fine of between 5000 Afs and 10,000 Afs.

(ii) Between 10 grams and 100g, imprisonment between six months and one year, and a fine of between 10,000 Afs and 50,000 Afs.

(iii) Between 100g and 500g, imprisonment for between one and three years, and a fine of between 50,000 and 100,000 Afs.

(iv) Between 500g and 1kg, imprisonment for between three and five years, and a fine of between 100,000 Afs and 500,000 Afs.

(v) Between 1kg and 5kg, imprisonment for between five and ten years, and a fine of between 500,000 Afs and 1,000,000 Afs.

(vi) Between 5kg and 50kg, imprisonment for between ten and fifteen years, and a fine of between 700,000 Afs and 1,500,000 Afs.

(vii) Over 50kg, life imprisonment and a fine of between 1,500,000 Afs and 5,000,000 Afs.

3. Whoever commits a drug trafficking offense involving the following quantities of the substances or any mixture containing substances listed in Tables 1 through 4, with the exception of heroin, morphine, cocaine, and opium, shall be sentenced as follows:

(i) Less than 250 grams, imprisonment for up to three months, and a fine of between 5000 Afs and 10,000 Afs.

(ii) Between 250 grams and 500g, imprisonment for between three months and six months and a fine of between 10,000 Afs and 50,000 Afs.

(iii) Between 500g and 1 kg, imprisonment for between six months and 1 year, and a fine of between 50,000 Afs and 100,000 Afs.

(iv) Between 1kg and 5kg, imprisonment for between one and three years, and a fine of between 100,000 Afs and 500,000 Afs.

(v) Between 5kg and 10kg, imprisonment for between five and ten years and a fine of between 500,000 Afs and up to 1,000,000 Afs.

(vi) Over 10kg, imprisonment for between ten and fifteen years, and a fine of between1, 000,000Afs and 1,500,000 Afs.[22]

4. Any person who, during the course of any of the offenses set forth in paragraphs 1, 2, and 3 of this article, directs, controls, organizes, finances, or guides three or more persons, shall be sentenced to penalties thrice as severe as the maximum penalties prescribed for that crime under the sub-paragraphs of paragraphs 1, 2, and 3 of this article, provided that the term of imprisonment does not exceed 20 years.

Article 17:

Aggregation of Amounts

1. If several persons are responsible for the commission of a drug trafficking offense, and the amounts of drugs trafficked by each of them is known, each of the offenders shall be punished under the provisions of this law pursuant to his share in the overall amount trafficked.

2. If several persons are responsible for the commission of a drug trafficking offense, but the share of each in the amount of drug trafficked is not known, each of them shall be sentenced to a penalty prescribed for the total amount trafficked.

Article 18:

Conspiracy, Aiding, Abetting, Facilitation, Incitement Any person who attempts, conspires, or engages in preparatory acts to commit any offense under this law shall be subject to the same penalties as the principal offender.

Article 19:

Drug laboratories, manufacturing, and storage

Whoever without authorization under this law opens, maintains, manages, or controls any property, building, room, or facility, as an owner, lessee, manager, agent, employee, or mortgagee, and intentionally rents, leases, or makes available for use, with or without compensation, such a place for the purpose of cultivating, manufacturing, processing, storing, concealing, or distributing any substance or mixture listed in Tables 1 through 4, or participates in or obtains an income from such activity, shall be sentenced to a term of imprisonment between 10 and 20 years and a fine of between 500,000Af. and 1,000,000 Afgs.

Article 20:

Importation or use of equipment for drug trafficking

1. Whoever imports equipment or materials used in or for the production and processing of regulated drugs without having a license, shall be sentenced to imprisonment for 5 to 10 years and a fine of between 100,000 and 500,000 Afs, and shall have the equipment or materials confiscated.[23]

2. Whoever lawfully imports equipment or materials used in or for the production and processing of drugs but uses them in the illicit production or processing of the regulated drugs, shall be sentenced to imprisonment for 10 to 15 years and a fine of between 500,000 and 1,000,000 Afs, and shall have the equipment or materials confiscated.

3. Whoever possesses or uses the equipment or materials referred to in paragraph 1 of this article for the illicit production or processing of regulated drugs, shall be sentenced to imprisonment for 15 to 20 years and a fine of between 1,000,000 and 2,000,000 Afs, and shall have the equipment and materials confiscated.

Article 21:

Drug-related corruption and intimidation

1. Any public official who intentionally commits one of the following acts shall be sentenced to imprisonment for 5 to 10 years and shall be fined twice the amount of the bribe:

(a) facilitating or assisting any offense under this law;

(b) obstructing an official investigation of an offense under this law or obstructing a trial of any offense under this law, including by failing to carry out lawful obligations; or

(c) directly or indirectly demanding, seeking, receiving, accepting, or agreeing to accept or receive a bribe in relation to drug trafficking or any official duty connected directly or indirectly to drug law enforcement,

A bribe-giver and a bribe-agent shall be sentenced to the same penalties as the bribe-taker.

2. Any person who threatens or intimidates another for the purpose of committing the following acts shall be sentenced to imprisonment between 5 and 8 years and fined between 500,000 and 1,000,000 Afs.

(a) committing or facilitating an offense under this law; or

(b) impeding a drug trafficking investigation or prosecution,

3. Any person who receives or accepts any benefit for the purpose of impeding or interfering with an investigation or criminal trial of a drug trafficking offense shall be sentenced to imprisonment for between 5 and 10 years, and shall relinquish the benefit.

4. Any person who threatens or seeks to intimidate any public official in connection with the detection of any drug trafficking offense, or an investigation or criminal[24] trial of any drug trafficking offense, shall be sentenced to imprisonment for between 5 and 10 years, and a fine of between 1,000,000Afs and 2,000,000 Afs.

5. Any person who injures any public official in connection with the detection, investigation or criminal trial of any drug trafficking offense, shall be sentenced to imprisonment between 10 to 15 years, and a fine of between 1,000,000Afs and 3,000,000 Afs.

6. Subject to the provisions of Chapter Seven of the Penal Code, the penalties set forth in paragraphs 1, 2, 3, 4, and 5 of this article shall be in addition to other penalties that an offender may be sentenced to for committing other criminal offenses.

Article 22:

Use of Weapons

1. Any person who uses, or causes the use of, any weapon during or in relation to any drug trafficking offense shall be punished by a term of five to ten years imprisonment, and a fine between 500,000 Afs and 1000,000 Afs.

2. Any person who carries or possesses any weapon, or causes another person to carry or possess any weapon, during or in relation to any drug trafficking offense shall be punished by a term of 3 to 5 years imprisonment, and a fine of between 500,000 Afs and 1,000,000 Afs.

Article 23:

Intimidation Leading to Drug-related Offenses

Any person who intentionally commits the following acts shall be sentenced to a term of imprisonment of between 5 and 8 years, and a fine of between 50,000 Afs and 200,000 Afs.

(a) Compelling another by force or intimidation to cultivate, manufacture, distribute, possess, sell, transport, store, or use substances or any mixture containing substances on Tables 1 through 4;

(b) Mixing substances on Tables 1 through 4 in food or drink intending that they be consumed by others;

(c) Distributing or sells any substance or mixture containing substances on Tables 1 through 4 to a child or to a person with mental health problems;

(d) Distributing any substance or mixture containing substances on Tables 1 through 4 in educational, military training, health or social service centers, or prisons;[25]

(e) Employing or using a child to commit a drug trafficking offense; or

(f) Allowing the consumption of substances or any mixture containing substances on Tables 1 through 4 in restaurants, hotels, shops or any other premises.

Article 24:

Illicit Prescription of Drugs

Any person who intentionally commits the following acts shall be sentenced to a term of imprisonment of between 3 and 5 years, and a fine of between 50,000 Afs and 100,000 Afs.

(a) Prescribing a regulated drug knowing it is to be used illegally; or

(b) Selling and buying regulated drugs using fraudulent prescriptions,

Article 25

Prohibition on Cultivation

1. Planting or cultivating opium poppy and seeds, coca bush, and cannabis plants within Afghanistan is a criminal offense and prohibited.

2. The owners, occupiers, or cultivators of lands are obligated to destroy opium poppy, coco bush, and cannabis plants growing on their lands. If they fail to do so shall be punished pursuant to the provisions of Article 26.

Article 26:

Penalties for Cultivation

1. Whoever plants or cultivates less than 1 jerib of opium poppy or coca bush without having a license shall be sentenced to a term of imprisonment between 6 months and 1 year and a fine between 10,000 Afs and 50,000 Afs.

2. Whoever plants or cultivates 1 jerib or more of opium poppy or coca bush shall, for each "beswa" (100 square meters) in excess of 1 jerib, be sentenced to imprisonment for 1 month and fine of 5,000 Afs, which penalty shall be in addition to the penalty prescribed in paragraph 1 of this article.

3. Whoever plants or cultivates less than 1 jerib of cannabis plants shall be sentenced to imprisonment for 3 to 9 months and a fine between 5,000 and 20,000 Afs.

4. Whoever plants or cultivates more than 1 jerib of cannabis plants, shall, for each beswa in excess of 1 jerib, be sentenced to imprisonment for 15 days and a fine of[26] 2,500 Afs, which penalty shall be in addition to the penalty prescribed in paragraph 3 of this article.

5. Whoever encourages, causes, incites, or finances any person to plant or cultivate opium poppy, coca bush, or cannabis plants shall be sentenced to twice the penalties of the farmer in accordance with the provisions of paragraphs 1, 2, 3, and 4 of this article.

6. Illicit opium poppy, coca bush, or cannabis plants shall be destroyed and any person associated with the cultivation or planting shall not be entitled to any compensation, in addition to the penalties set forth in this article.

Article 27:

Consumption of illegal drugs, and treatment of dependant persons or addicts

1. Any person who uses or possesses for the purpose of personal consumption any substance or mixture containing a substance listed in Tables 1 through 4, other than as authorized for medical treatment or by this law, shall be punished as follows:

(a) Heroin, morphine, and cocaine, or any mixture containing those substances: 6 months to 1 year imprisonment and a fine between 20,000 to 50,000 Afs.

(b) Opium or any mixture containing that substance: 3 months to 6 months imprisonment and a fine of between 10,000 Afs to 25,000 Afs.

(c) Substances or any mixture containing substances listed in Tables 1 through 4, with the exception of those in paragraphs 1 and 2 of this article: 1 month to 3 months imprisonment and a fine of between 5,000 Afs to 10,000 Afs.

(d) Possession of more than 1 gram of heroin, morphine, or cocaine, or 10 grams of opium or hashish, shall be subject to the penalties set forth in Article 16.

2. If a medical doctor certifies that a person is addicted to an illegal drug substance listed in Tables 1 through 4, the court may exempt the person from imprisonment and fine. In this case, the court may require an addicted person to attend a detoxification or drug treatment center.

3. Detoxification or drug treatment centers shall report to the sentencing court through the office of the prosecutor every 15 days on the health condition of persons sentenced to detention and treatment. On the basis of the report received, the court can abrogate or extend the period of detention and treatment.[27]

4. Any person sentenced to a period of detention in a detoxification or drug treatment center shall receive credit on any sentence of imprisonment for the time served in the treatment center.

5. Any person in control of a vehicle while under the influence of any narcotic or psychotropic substance listed in Tables 1 through 3 shall be sentenced to a term of imprisonment of between six months and one year and a fine of 10,000 to 20,000 Afs.

Article 28:

Vehicles

1. Whoever without legal authorization intentionally carries, transports, or conceals more than 10 grams of heroin, morphine, or cocaine; or more than 20 grams of opium; or more than 100 grams of hashish or any other substance listed in Tables

1 through 4 in his vehicle shall have the vehicle confiscated, in addition to the punishment prescribed in this law.

2. Any vehicle owner who without legal authorization intentionally allows a vehicle to be used to carry, transport, or conceal more than 10 grams of heroin, morphine, or cocaine; or more than 20 grams of opium; or more than 100 grams of hashish or any other substance listed in Tables 1 through 4 shall be punished as an accomplice to the crime and shall have the vehicle confiscated.

3. Any vehicle seized in relation to a drug-trafficking offense shall be registered and officially handed over to the nearest customs office and following the completion of its confiscation in accordance with the provisions of the relevant law, it shall be placed on sale and the proceeds be deposited to the government treasury.

Article 29:

Repeat offenders

If any person who has been convicted more than once of an offense listed in Articles 16,18,19, 20, 21, 22, 23, 24, 25, 26, 27, or 28 of this law commits a narcotics offense again, he shall be sentenced to the maximum penalty provided for that offense.

Article 30:

Home Leave

The provisions of Article 37 of the Law of Prisons and Detention Centres shall not apply to those who have committed crimes prescribed in this law and have been sentenced to a term of more than 5 years imprisonment.[28]

Article 31:

Penalty Aggravation

1. Except as provided for under this law, the penalty aggravation provisions of the Penal Code shall apply to violent actions of drug-trafficking offenders. 2. The provisions of other laws with regard to the suspension of sentences, judicial leniency, and probation shall not apply to convicts of drug-trafficking offenses.

Article 32:

Licensing and Reporting Violations

Whoever does not comply with the provisions of this law and the relevant regulation on the issuance of licenses, authorizations or reporting, and provides for the issuance of a license or an authorization knowing that it will be abused, shall be sentenced to 6 months to 1 year imprisonment and a fine between 50,000 and 100,000 Afs. If the person repeats the violation, he shall be sentenced to 1 to 3 years imprisonment and a fine between 150,000 and 350,000 Afs.

Article 33:

Commission on the Assessment of Drug-Related Offenses and Penalties

1. In order to study and assess the patterns of drug-trafficking offenses across the country, the Commission on the Assessment of Drug-Related Offenses and Penalties (hereinafter the Commission) shall be established with the following composition:

a. One authorized representative from the Supreme Court;

b. One authorized representative from the Office of the Attorney General;

c. One authorized representative from the Ministry of Counter-Narcotics;

d. One authorized representative from the Ministry of Interior;

e. One authorized representative from the Ministry of Public Health;

f. One authorized representative from the National Security Directorate;

g. One defense lawyer appointed by the Minister of Justice.

Members of the Commission shall be appointed for a period of four years and shall elect one from among themselves as Chairperson for a two-year term.

3. The Commission shall have the following duties and authorities:

a. Studying and assessing the patterns of drug-trafficking offenses in the country and collecting the relevant data;

b. Preparing proposals on the amendment of the provisions of this law on drug-related offenses and penalties on the basis of the data collected on the [29] offenses and presenting the same, through the Ministry of CounterNarcotics, to the Government within 60 days of their development;

c. Recording the committed drug-trafficking offenses;

d. Preparing an annual report on drug-trafficking offenses and presenting it to the Government;

e. Holding hearing sessions for considering possible changes in the penalties prescribed for drug-related offenses.

4. The administrative costs of the Commission and its secretariat shall be funded from the budget of the Ministry of Counter-Narcotics. The Ministry shall also pay an appropriate salary to the defense lawyer and appropriate attendance fees to other members of the Commission.

5. Citizens of Afghanistan may freely file their complaints on drug-related offenses with the Commission. Reviewing complaints, holding meetings and other activities of the Commission shall be regulated through procedures adopted by the Commission.

6. Any amendment to this law proposed by the Commission shall be presented to the National Assembly following its approval by the Government.[30]

CHAPTER V

Adjudication of drug-related offenses

Article 34:

Narcotics Tribunals

1. In accordance with the provisions of Articles 32 and 50 of the Law Concerning the Organization and Jurisdiction of Courts of the Islamic Republic of Afghanistan, a Narcotics Tribunal within the Kabul Primary Provincial Court and a Narcotics Tribunal within the Kabul Appellate Provincial Court are hereby established.

2. Each of the tribunals set forth in paragraph 1 of this article shall be composed of one President and six members.

3. The Presidents of the tribunals shall be responsible for leading and managing the affairs of their respective tribunals and shall preside over judicial proceedings in accordance with the provisions of Articles 37 and 43 of the Law Concerning the Organization and Jurisdiction of Courts of the Islamic Republic of Afghanistan.

4. The tribunals set forth in paragraph 1 of this article shall exercise exclusive jurisdiction throughout Afghanistan over drug trafficking offenses in the following cases:

(a) Two or more kgs. of heroin, morphine, or cocaine, or any mixture containing those substances;

(b) Ten or more kgs. of opium or any mixture containing opium; and

(c) Fifty or more kgs. of hashish or any mixture containing substances listed in Tables 1 through 4, with the exception of heroin, morphine, cocaine, and opium.

5. If the amount of narcotic drugs is less than those set forth in paragraph 4 of this article, the case comes under jurisdiction of the Public Security Tribunals of Provincial Courts.

6. Adjudication of drug-related offenses shall be in conformity with the provisions of the Law Concerning the Organization and Jurisdiction of Courts of the Islamic Republic of Afghanistan and other relevant laws.

7. The appointment of the Judges of the Central Narcotics Tribunals and the regulation of other affairs related to their promotion and retirement shall be conducted in accordance with the provisions of the Law Concerning the Organization and Jurisdiction of Courts of the Islamic Republic of Afghanistan.[31]

8. The amounts and types of narcotic drugs set forth in paragraph 4 over which the Narcotics Tribunals shall exercise exclusive jurisdiction throughout Afghanistan shall be subject to amendment in accordance with the procedures set forth in Article 33.

9. The Central Narcotics Tribunal shall also have jurisdiction over criminal offenses connected or related to drug trafficking offenses set forth in sub-paragraphs 1, 2, and 3 of paragraph 4 of this article.

Article 35:

Investigation, Prosecution, Trial, and Extradition

1. Investigation, prosecution, and the trial of persons involved in drug-trafficking offenses shall be carried out in accordance with the provisions of the Criminal Procedure Code and other relevant laws, and the penalties shall be prescribed in accordance with the provisions of this law. In case this law lacks the required provisions to decide on a penalty, the provisions of the Penal Code shall apply.

2. Suspects accused or convicted of drug trafficking offenses shall be extradited in accordance with the provisions of the 1988 United Nations Convention against Illicit Traffic in Narcotics Drugs and Psychotropic Substances, and in accordance with international agreements that may be signed with other countries.

Article 36:

Special Counter Narcotics Saranwal

1. The Office of the Attorney General shall create a Special Counter Narcotics Saranwal within its office to investigate and prosecute the offenses under this law.

2. The Special Counter Narcotics Saranwal shall have exclusive jurisdiction over investigation and prosecution of drug-trafficking offenses set forth in paragraph 4 of Article 34 of this law, and shall cooperate with other law enforcement officials in conducting their investigations.

3. The investigation and prosecution of drug-trafficking offenses involving amounts of drugs less than those set forth in paragraph 4 of article 34 of this law shall be the jurisdiction of other relevant Saranwalis in accordance with the provisions of law.

4. The appointment of the prosecutors and the handling of other affairs related to their promotion and retirement shall be carried out in accordance with the provisions of the law.[32]

Article 37:

Duties of the Counter Narcotics Police

1. The Counter Narcotics Police of Afghanistan and other law enforcement authorities referred to in paragraph 2 of this article shall be responsible for detecting drug trafficking offenses in Afghanistan.

2. The following law enforcement agencies may seize illegal drugs, drug crimes proceeds, and related materials and equipment:

(a) the Counter Narcotics Police;

(b) the Afghan Special Narcotics Force;

(c) the National Police;

(d) the Border Police;

(e) the Afghanistan Customs staff.

3. All seizures of illegal drug substances, evidence, and proceeds by any of the law enforcement agencies referred to in paragraph 2 of this article shall be reported immediately to the Counter Narcotics Police. The Counter Narcotics Police shall transmit the report as soon as practicable to the National Headquarters of the Counter Narcotics Police, the Ministry of Counter Narcotics, the Office of the Attorney General, and the Commission on the Assessment of Drug-Related Offenses and Penalties.

4. All seizures of illegal drug substances, evidence, and proceeds by any law enforcement authorities referred to in paragraph 2 of this article shall be turned over to the Counter Narcotics Police as soon as practicable.

5. Law enforcement agencies referred to in paragraph 2 of this article shall, at the request of Counter Narcotics Police, provide additional security to protect seized drugs, evidence, proceeds, and suspects.

6. The Counter Narcotics Police shall have the authority to question and interrogate all the perpetrators of the drug-trafficking offenses under this law.

7. The Counter Narcotics Police of Afghanistan shall refer perpetrators of the offenses under paragraph 4 of Article 34 of this law to the Special Counter Narcotics Saranwal for investigation and prosecution. If the amount of drugs seized is less than those set under paragraph 4 of article 34 of this law, the respective cases shall be referred to the concerned Saranwalis for investigation and judicial prosecution. [33]

8. If the amount of drugs seized is less than those set under paragraph 4 of Article 34 of this law, the law enforcement agencies named under paragraph 2 of this article shall complete the questioning and interrogation of the suspects within 72 hours and refer the concerned cases to the respective Saranwalis for investigation and judicial prosecution.

9. In cases where a seizure of quantities of narcotic drugs as set under paragraph 4 of Article 34 of this law is made outside Kabul Province and the offenders are arrested, the law enforcement agencies referred to in paragraph 2 of this article shall have up to, but not longer than, 72 hours from the time of arrest to prepare a report of the arrest and turn the accused over to the Primary Saranwal. As soon as possible, but not longer than 15 days after the arrest, the Counter Narcotics Police shall transfer the investigation, the evidence, and the accused to the Headquarters of the Counter Narcotics Police in Kabul for further questioning and interrogation.

The time period for the questioning and interrogation of the accused shall begin upon the date the accused physically arrives in Kabul in the custody of the Counter Narcotics Police, but the time period for the turning over of the accused to the Special Counter Narcotics Saranwal shall in no event exceed 15 days from the date of arrest. The Special Narcotics Saranwal, upon being notified, shall inform the Primary Central Narcotics Tribunal in Kabul of such arrests outside Kabul Province, and obtain an order from the Court extending the dates for indictment. It shall investigate and prosecute the case in accordance with the provisions set forth in Article 36 of the Interim Criminal Procedure Code.

Article 38:

Reports on drug seizures

1. A report shall be prepared by the person responsible for the seizure of illegal drugs and shall contain the following information:

(a) The type of illegal drug seized, and a physical description of the seizure, including any packaging containing the drugs;

(b) The quantity of illegal drugs seized;

(c) The time, date and place of the seizure;

(d) The organization and person responsible for the seizure;

(e) The name, date of birth, address, and signature and fingerprints of any person arrested in connection with the seizure;

(f) A factual description of the circumstances of the seizure.

2. The report shall be signed by the person responsible for the seizure and a member of the Counter Narcotics Police if present. One copy of the report shall be kept by[34] each of the signatories to the report. Additional copies shall be submitted to the Saranwal for inclusion in the investigation dossier, and to the Ministry of Counter Narcotics.

Article 39:

Destruction of illegal drugs and preservation of evidence

The illegal drugs seized shall be destroyed in accordance with the following procedures:

(a) All drugs seized shall be turned over to the custody of the Counter

Narcotics Police as soon as possible.

(b) Authorized representatives of the Counter Narcotics Police and the concerned Saranwal shall weigh and photograph the entire amount seized, and take samples of the drugs for testing, in accordance with written procedures which shall be established by the Attorney General. The Ministry of Counter Narcotics, or its provincial offices, shall be informed about this sampling process.

(c) After samples of the drugs are taken, the remaining drugs shall be reweighed to ensure that the original amount seized is not less than it was after the sample was taken.

(d) The Saranwal shall issue a written order authorizing the destruction of the drugs after they have been photographed, sampled, and reweighed.

(e) Representatives of the Counter Narcotics Police and the Saranwal shall prepare and sign an exact report containing the information required under this article and keep a record of the same.

(f) The Counter Narcotics Police shall destroy the remaining illegal drugs as soon as possible in the presence of representatives of the Saranwal. The Ministry of Counter Narcotics shall be advised of and may participate in this process.

Article 40:

Afghan Special Narcotics Force

1. A Special Narcotics Force is established within the Ministry of Interior to detain those involved in drug trafficking, to seize illegal drugs, and to use reasonable force in the conduct of its operations, including against those who impede its operations.

2. The Special Narcotics Force shall hand over any suspects and evidence in its custody associated with a drug seizure to the Counter Narcotics Police of Afghanistan pursuant to the procedures set forth in Articles 37, 38, and 39.[35]

3. The Special Narcotics Force shall have the power to destroy illegal drugs, if necessary.

Article 41:

Co-operation with law enforcement agencies

1. If an accused cooperates considerably with the responsible authorities in investigation and trial in detecting or arresting other perpetrators, the prosecutor can request to sentence the accused to up to 50% of the minimum penalty prescribed for the perpetrated crime.

2. Any person who provides authentic information relating to drug trafficking offenses or offenders, or arrests, or assists in the arrest of, the offenders may be awarded money, depending on the circumstances and the quality and quantity of the drugs seized, at the discretion of the Counter Narcotics Police and in accordance with guidelines which shall be established by the Ministry of Interior.

Article 42:

Confiscation of Assets

1. No person may retain any benefits or assets, whether immovable or movable, acquired directly or indirectly by the commission of a criminal offense under this law.

2. The prosecutor shall provide sufficient evidence in support of the confiscation of benefits or assets in accordance with paragraph 1 of this Article. The court shall consider any evidence produced by the accused to refute the evidence produced by the prosecutor, and shall order confiscation only after it is certain that benefits or assets were acquired directly or indirectly as the result of the commission of a criminal offense under this law.

3. Benefits and immovable or movable assets that may be confiscated or forfeited as a result of the commission of a criminal offense under this law shall include the following:

(a) Facilities, material, equipment, movable or immovable assets, funds or any other objects of value directly or indirectly used or intended to be used in committing the crime.

(b) Money, funds, objects of material value, and any other income acquired directly or indirectly through committing the crime.

(c) Moveable or immovable materials purchased or acquired with the proceeds or income of the crime.[36]

(d) Salary or other privileges received by legal or natural persons in connection with the crime.

4. When funds or assets ordered to be confiscated are not available, funds or assets of equivalent value shall be ordered to be confiscated. This order shall be applicable to funds or assets belonging directly or indirectly to the perpetrators of the offenses under this law.

5. If the funds or assets whose confiscation has been ordered have been transferred to another person, the transferred funds or assets shall be confiscated, provided that the person to whom the funds or assets have been transferred was aware of the origin of the funds or assets.

6. If the transferee did not know that the funds or assets transferred to him had been acquired by the commission of a criminal offense under this law, he shall have the right to present evidence of his lack of knowledge on this regard to the court.[37]

Chapter VI

Search, Seizure, and Investigation Techniques

Article 43:

Detection, Investigation, and Prosecution

The provisions of this Chapter shall apply to the detection, investigation, and prosecution of drug trafficking and drug trafficking-related offenses, including offenses involving bribery and corruption, violence, and money laundering.

Article 44:

Search of Person

1. Law enforcement authorities search a person where there are justifiable reasons to believe that evidence and forfeitable objects or instruments and funds related to drug-trafficking are concealed on or in the suspect's clothing or body.

2. A strip-search may only be conducted by a law enforcement officer of the same sex. Internal examinations of body orifices may only be carried out by an authorized medical examiner after approval by a local court. Where an individual consents to a body search, the authorization from a court is not needed.

3. Any object or article reasonably relevant to criminal activity may be seized during a search of a person. A record of the reasons for and circumstances of the search, the name of the Judge or other authorizing officer, where applicable, and the disposition of any seized items shall be made. This record can be produced in the future legal proceedings.

4. Evidence properly obtained as a result of a search shall be admissible in all court and other legal proceedings.

Article 45:

Search of Property

1. Law enforcement authorities may enter and search private residences after obtaining a warrant from a relevant court.

2. Convincing reasons that justify the search, and the exact address of the property to be searched, should be explicitly mentioned in the search warrant application.

3. A court may issue a search warrant where there is reasonable cause to believe that evidence, instrumentalities, or proceeds of drug-trafficking or of other offenses, are stored, maintained, or concealed in or on the premises to be searched. If the owner or the resident of the property consents to a search, there is no need for the court authorization.[38]

4. In exceptional circumstances where there is reasonable cause to believe that evidence, instrumentalities, or proceeds of criminal activity or offenses may be removed or destroyed and the issuance of a search warrant by a court is not possible, law enforcement officers may act pursuant to the provisions of the Criminal Procedure Code.

5. Law enforcement officers may seize all evidence, instrumentalities, or proceeds of criminal activities or offenses, including records maintained in any form, format, or medium, specified in the warrant and are related to drug trafficking offenses. A record of the reasons for and circumstances of the search, the name of the judge or other authorizing officer, where applicable, and the disposition of any seized items shall be made and maintained for all future legal proceedings. Where a search warrant was not obtained prior to a search because of exceptional circumstances, the record shall also include a description of such exceptional circumstances and the attempts made to contact a Sarwanal before the search.

6. Evidence properly obtained pursuant to a search warrant or consent shall be admissible in all court and other legal proceedings. Law enforcement officers shall, following entering and searching a property, obtain a court order establishing the legality of their action within a period of time as set under the law.

Article 46:

Search of Vehicles

1. Law enforcement authorities may stop and search a vehicle where there is reasonable cause to believe that evidence, instrumentalities, or proceeds of drug trafficking offenses are stored, maintained, or concealed on or within the vehicle, its load, or any trailer.

2. Law enforcement authorities may seize the vehicle and any evidence, instrumentalities, or proceeds of drug-trafficking offenses, including records maintained in any form, format or medium, relevant to such criminal activities or offenses. A record of the reasons for and circumstances of the search and the disposition of any seized items shall be made and maintained for all future legal proceedings. Evidence properly obtained pursuant to an authorized vehicle search shall be admissible in all court and other legal proceedings.

Article 47:

Covert Surveillance

1. Law enforcement authorities and their authorized agents may conduct covert investigative and surveillance activities to gather intelligence and evidence of criminal activities or offenses. Covert investigative and surveillance activities may include:[39]

• recording conversations in public places;

• conducting mobile or static surveillance with or without the use of electronic or photographic equipment;

• collecting data related to using, providing, and transmitting telecommunications and other electronic communications, pursuant to written regulations that shall be established by the Attorney General;

• controlled deliveries of prohibited or other items.

2. A record of the covert surveillance conducted shall be kept.

3. Evidence properly gained through the authorized use of covert investigative and surveillance methods shall be admissible in all court and other legal proceedings.

Article 48:

Intrusive or Electronic Surveillance

1. Law enforcement authorities and their authorized agents may conduct intrusive investigative and electronic surveillance activities during and in connection with efforts to gather intelligence and evidence relevant to the commission of drug trafficking offenses. Intrusive or electronic surveillance methods may include:

• overt or covert recording of conversations in private property, places, and residences;

• installation and use of electronic or photographic equipment in or on private property, places, or residences;

• interception of communications, including voice, data and internet communications, conversations and information transmitted by electronic means or media by, from, or through telecommunications companies, internet and computer service providers, or other electronic communications service providers;

• inspecting bank accounts and records of financial transactions or transfers; and

• opening and inspecting mail.

2. Evidence properly obtained through the authorized use of overt or covert intrusive investigative and electronic surveillance methods shall be admissible in all court and other legal proceedings.[40]

3. In all cases under this article, the confidentiality of the conversations, mailings, and communications between the accused and his lawyer shall be kept immune from any form of intrusion.

Article 49:

Electronic Interception and Surveillance Standards

1. With the exception of law enforcement agencies or their agents, any person who intentionally —

(a) intercepts any wire, oral, or electronic communication;

(b) uses any electronic, mechanical, or other device to intercept any oral communication;

(c) discloses to any other person the contents of any wire, oral, or electronic communication, knowing that the information was obtained through the interception of a wire, oral, or electronic communication in violation of this Article;

(d) uses the contents of any wire, oral, or electronic communication, knowing that the information was obtained through the interception of a wire, oral, or electronic communication in violation of this Article; or

(e) discloses to any other person the contents of any wire, oral, or electronic communication, intercepted by means authorized by this Article,

(i) knowing that the information was obtained through the interception of such a communication in connection with a criminal investigation,

(ii) having obtained or received the information in connection with a criminal investigation, and

(iii) with intent to improperly obstruct, impede, or interfere with a duly authorized criminal investigation, shall be subject to 1 to 5 years imprisonment and a fine of between 20,000 and 100,000 Afs.

2. It shall not be unlawful for an officer, employee, or agent of a provider of wire or electronic communication service, whose facilities are used in the transmission of a wire

or electronic communication, to intercept, disclose, or use that communication in the normal course of his employment.

3. A person or entity providing an electronic communication service to the public shall not intentionally divulge the contents of any communication to any person or [41] entity other than an addressee or intended recipient of such communication or an agent of such addressee or intended recipient, except -

(i) as authorized in this Article;

(ii) with the lawful consent of the originator or any addressee or intended recipient of such communication;

(iii) to a person employed or authorized, or whose facilities are used, to forward such communication to its destination; or

(iv) the communications were inadvertently obtained by the service provider and which appear to pertain to the commission of a crime, if such divulgence is made to a law enforcement agency.

4. Whenever any wire or oral communication has been intercepted, no part of the contents of such communication and no evidence derived there from shall be admissible as evidence in any trial, hearing, or other proceeding or before any other official authority if the disclosure of that information would be in violation of this Article.

5. The consent of one of the parties to the communication shall constitute authorization for surveillance, interception, or inspection of communications and information under this Article.

6. An application for the interception of communications shall be prepared by a Saranwal and approved by an authorized official of the Office of the Attorney General. The application shall specify the reasons to believe that:

(a) the named suspects and others are engaged in the commission of drug trafficking or drug-related offenses;

(b) the named suspects and others are using a particular telephone or premises in connection with the commission of the offenses;

(c) that wire and/or oral communications of the named suspects and others will be intercepted either over the particular telephone facility and/or within the described premises;

(d) the time for which the interception is required to be maintained; and

(e) where the application is for the extension of a previous order, a statement setting forth the results thus far obtained from the interception, or a reasonable explanation of the failure to obtain such results.

7. The application for and authorization of surveillance or interception under this section should be in writing but may be made orally if there are urgent or emergency circumstances. The application to conduct an interception shall include sufficient information to justify the use of the type of interception sought.[42] The court issuing the Order shall state any conditions or limits to the planned interception or surveillance in the Order authorizing the application. Urgent oral applications and authorizations require the same information and justification as written ones. Written applications and authorizations will be made as soon as practicable following oral authorization and will state the need for urgency.

8. Each Order authorizing or approving the interception of any wire, oral, or electronic communication under this chapter shall specify—

(a) the identity of the person, if known, whose communications are to be intercepted;

(b) the nature and location of the communications facilities as to which, or the place where, authority to intercept is granted;

(c) a particular description of the type of communication sought to be intercepted, and a statement of the particular offense to which it relates;

(d) the identity of the agency authorized to intercept the communications, and of the person approving the application; and

(e) the period of time during which such interception is authorized, including a statement as to whether or not the interception shall automatically terminate when the described communication has been first obtained.

9. An Interception Order is valid until the objectives authorized in the Order are attained or 60 days from the day on which the law enforcement officers first begin to conduct an interception under the Order. It shall be renewable for additional 60 day periods upon a showing of continued necessity for interception.

10. The authorization given shall apply to the target telephone number as well as any changed telephone number within the 60 day period. If the telephone is a cellular telephone, the authorization applies both to the target telephone number as well as any changed telephone number or any other telephone number subsequently assigned to or used by the instrument bearing the same electronic serial number as the target cellular phone within the 60 day period.

11. Monitoring personnel may listen only to criminal conversations, and must turn off the interception devices when the parties to the conversation engage in noncriminal conversations.

12. The recordings of the intercepted communications shall be sealed in a container and taken to the court which issued the interception order within 30 days of the end of the

authorized interception period in order to protect the recordings from tampering or destruction and to ensure that the contents are not unlawfully disclosed.[43]

13. No provider of wire or electronic communication service, officer, employee, or agent thereof shall disclose the existence of any interception or surveillance or the device used to accomplish the interception or surveillance with respect to which the person has been furnished a court order under this Article, except in case of exigency and then only after prior notification to the Attorney General.

14. When a law enforcement officer intercepts wire, oral, or electronic communications relating to offenses other than those specified in the Interception Order, the contents thereof, and evidence derived there from, may be disclosed or used for law enforcement purposes, or disclosed under oath in any proceeding, when the judge finds on subsequent application that the contents were otherwise intercepted in accordance with this Article and the original order. The court shall be notified as soon as practicable that conversations about other offenses are being monitored, and the new offenses shall be added to the original application for the order if an extension order is obtained. If no extension order is obtained and the prosecution wishes to use that evidence in a future proceeding, an order should be obtained as soon as practicable pursuant to this Article.

15. Disclosure of information obtained pursuant to a court-authorized interception order is authorized in the following circumstances:

• to law enforcement officers for the performance of their official duties. In this case, the law enforcement officers may use the information as required.

• information may be disclosed during testimony under oath.

16. Information regarding offenses other than those authorized in the order may be disclosed to other law enforcement officers with a court authorization. In this case, they may use the information as required.

17. A law enforcement officer may disclose interception information to other law enforcement, intelligence, protective, immigration, national defence, or national security officials, if the information includes intelligence or counterintelligence, to assist the receiving officials in the performance of their official duties.

18. A law enforcement officer, or other Government official engaged in carrying out official duties, may disclose the contents of intercepted communications and evidence derived there from to foreign or domestic investigative or law enforcement officers if such disclosure is appropriate to the proper performance of the official duties of the officers who disclose and who receive the information.

Foreign investigative or law enforcement officers may use or disclose such contents or derivative evidence to the extent appropriate to the performance of their official duties.[44]

19. If the contents of intercepted communications or derivative evidence reveals a threat of actual or potential attack or other grave hostile acts of a foreign power or an agent of a foreign power, sabotage, terrorism, or clandestine intelligence gathering activities by an intelligence service or network of a foreign power or by an agent of a foreign power, within Afghanistan or elsewhere, a law enforcement officer, or other Government official engaged in carrying out official duties, may disclose the contents of intercepted communications and evidence derived there from to any appropriate Government or foreign government official, for the purpose of preventing or responding to such threat. The foreign official who receives such information may use it consistent with such guidelines as the Office of the Attorney General and the National Security Directorate (NDS) shall jointly issue.

20. The Interception Order issued by the judge may provide in appropriate circumstances and for good cause that the order be sealed, and the surveillance or interception conducted not be disclosed until the conclusion of the investigation or until further order of the court. The order of the court may specify that the methods, means, and techniques used in the interception or surveillance remain secret.

21. The Interception Order issued by the judge may permit law enforcement officers to surreptitiously enter the premises to be shrivelled at any time to install or replace a recording or surveillance device, or replace the battery.

22. Communications service providers shall allow designated law enforcement authorities access, as per the Interception Order, to the content of the specified communications at the time of transmission or as soon as practicable thereafter, and shall cooperate with law enforcement authorities in the installation or connection of all technical equipment necessary to the interception and recordation of the communications. Communications service providers and their employees and agents are forbidden to disclose the installation of interception equipment.

Article 50:

Use of Informants

1. Law enforcement authorities may use informants to prevent, detect, and investigate drug-trafficking offenses by gathering intelligence and evidence relevant to the commission of such offenses.

2. An informant may establish or maintain a relationship with a person in order to acquire information or evidence of illegal activities and to provide that information and evidence to law enforcement authorities. Informants may use surveillance techniques described in this Article if authorized by appropriate law enforcement authorities.[45]

3. Informants may not participate in the commission of drug-trafficking offenses in connection with criminal investigations without prior authorization from the appropriate law enforcement authorities. An informant who conducts or participates in criminal

activity outside the limit of the authorized conduct may be subject to prosecution for any offense committed.

4. Authorizations for informants to acquire information or participate in crimes shall be recorded in writing and shall specify to the extent practicable the types of actions the informant may engage in or conduct. All information provided by an informant shall be recorded by the officer receiving it.

5. The identity of an informant may be withheld by an order of a court where there is reasonable cause to believe that identifying the informant will subject him to danger or compromise lawful investigations. The order issued by the court may provide in appropriate circumstances that the order be sealed and not be disclosed to another party until the conclusion of the investigation or until further order of the court, and that the methods, means, and techniques used in the investigation remain secret.

6. An informant may testify in court.

7. Evidence properly gained through the authorized use of informants shall be admissible in all detection, investigation, and trial proceedings.

8. Informants shall be recruited in accordance with special procedures established by the Ministry of Interior.

Article 51:

Undercover Operations

1. Law enforcement authorities may conduct undercover or covert operations during and in connection with investigations to gather intelligence and evidence relevant to the commission of drug-trafficking offenses. Undercover or covert operations and methods may include purchasing, selling, or offering to purchase or sell, illicit drugs and controlled substances, or other activities. Undercover or covert operations and methods shall not be used to initiate crimes that would [not] otherwise have been committed. A record of all undercover or covert operations conducted shall be made and maintained.

2. Intelligence includes information relevant to the detection and prevention of drug trafficking offenses. The source of intelligence may be protected.

3. Evidence properly obtained through the authorized use of undercover or covert operations shall be admissible in all detection, investigation, and trial proceedings.[46]

CHAPTER VII

Duties and Responsibilities of the Ministry of Counter Narcotics and other

Ministries

Article 52:

Duties and responsibilities

1. The Ministry of Counter Narcotics shall coordinate the counter-narcotics activities and programs of the Government of Afghanistan with other Ministries, independent bodies, and other concerned organizations.

2. The Ministry of Counter Narcotics, as the leading Ministry in counter narcotics affairs, shall be responsible for coordinating and evaluating the implementation of this Law and the National Drug Control Strategy in the concerned Ministries and organizations, and shall adopt the necessary measures for this purpose in the relevant central and provincial offices.

3. The concerned Ministries and organizations shall present a report, on a monthly basis or upon request, on their counter-narcotic activities to the Ministry of Counter Narcotics.

4. The Ministry of Counter Narcotics shall submit to the Government a quarterly report on the results obtained from the evaluation of the activities and performances of the concerned organizations in combating narcotic drugs.

5. Ministries, agencies and other concerned organizations shall be responsible for the implementation of this law and the National Drug Control Strategy in their respective areas of activity.

6. The Minister for Counter Narcotics, assisted by other Ministries, and other bodies and institutions, shall prepare a National Drug Control Strategy (NDCS), and propose revisions to the strategy at regular intervals but not less than every three years. The Ministry shall be responsible for evaluating the implementation of the NDCS.

7. The Ministry of Counter Narcotics shall coordinate the annual budget of the National Drug Control Strategy with the Ministry of Finance. The Ministry of Counter Narcotics and the Ministry of Finance shall be jointly responsible for the management and implementation of the Counter Narcotics Trust Fund.

8. The Ministries of Counter Narcotics, Interior, Finance, National Defense and other Ministries, bodies and institutions, including but not limited to the Supreme Court, Office of the Attorney General, and National Directorate of Security, shall cooperate and assist one another as required to perform their lawful duties and functions under this law.[47]

Article 53:

Intelligence Duties

1. The National Directorate of Security shall obtain intelligence on drug cultivation, production, and trafficking, and shall prepare strategic and operational intelligence reports related to counter narcotics.

2. Strategic intelligence reports on counter narcotics shall be submitted on a regular basis to the Office of the National Security Adviser, the Ministry of Interior, and the Ministry of Counter Narcotics.

Article 54:

Duties of Other Ministries

1. The Ministry of Public Health, in consultation with the Ministry of Counter Narcotics, shall establish community-based and residential detoxification; harm reduction, treatment and rehabilitation services for persons addicted to or dependant on narcotic drugs and/or psychotropic substances.

2. The Ministry of Education and Ministry of Higher Education shall, in consultation with the Ministry of Counter Narcotics, include illicit drug use prevention-related subjects into the curriculum of their educational institutions.

3. The Ministries of Culture and Information, Public Health, Religious Affairs (Hajj and Awqaf) and other relevant bodies shall, in consultation with the Ministry of Counter Narcotics, promote public campaigns against illegal drug cultivation, production, trafficking, and use.

4. In accordance with the National Drug Control Strategy, and within their competence, the Ministries of Agriculture, Food Stuff and Animal Husbandry, Rural Rehabilitation and Development, Public Health, and Interior shall adopt measures to:

(i) Prevent opium poppy and cannabis cultivation through all possible means;

(ii) Persuade and encourage farmers to cultivate licit crops.

(iii) Provide assistance to farmers.

5. The Ministry of Foreign Affairs shall adopt measures to:

(i) Attract assistance from international organizations to assist farmers.

(ii) Acquire assistance from international organizations to equip and expand hospitals and rehabilitation centers for drug addicts.[48]

(iii) Collect reports, publications and information material related to the struggle against drugs from regional and international organizations, and translate and distribute them;

(iv) Initiate efforts to negotiate agreements with other countries and organizations regarding co-operation in detection, investigation, arrest, prosecution, trial, and extradition of drug-trafficking suspects.

(v) Negotiate agreements with other countries and international organizations for cooperation and technical and financial assistance to prevent opium, cannabis, and coca cultivation and to combat drug trafficking in Afghanistan.

(vi) Cooperate with the United Nations and other foreign authorities to prevent the manufacture of instruments, equipment, and machinery used for producing and processing narcotic drugs and psychotropic substances.

(vii) Present to the Secretary-General of the United Nations an annual report, drafted by the Ministry of Counter Narcotics, on the implementation of the international conventions on illegal drugs.

(viii) Exchange information and counter-narcotic activities with foreign countries and international organizations.

(ix) Establishing relations between the International Narcotics Control Board (INCB) and the Counter Narcotics Ministry and other relevant ministries and institutions.

(x) Designate, in consultation with the Counter Narcotics Ministry, Drug Liaison Officers (DLO) in neighbouring, regional and other interested countries.

(xi) Cooperate with the Counter Narcotics Ministry in holding regional and international conferences on counter-narcotic issues.

(xii) Consult with the Ministry of Counter Narcotics in formulating and implementing the duties and responsibilities set forth in this

paragraph.[49]

CHAPTER VIII

Final Provisions

Article 55:

Responsibility of Security Authorities

All security authorities shall be responsible for preventing and eradicating the cultivation of opium poppy, cannabis plants, and coca bush in accordance with the instructions of the Government.

Article 56:

Primacy of this law

1. Where existing laws and regulations conflict with this law, this law shall prevail.

All regulations that are incompatible with this law shall be conformed to this law no later than 6 months after the promulgation of this law.

2. The Counter Narcotics Ministry shall issue all regulations required by this law within one year of the promulgation of this law. Pending the promulgation of such regulations, the existing regulations concerning counter narcotics activities shall remain in force if such regulations are not inconsistent with this law.

Article 57:

Cooperation of Ministries

1. Within 60 days of the promulgation of this law, the Ministry of Counter Narcotics, with the assistance of the Ministry of Interior, shall take the measures necessary to meet the organizational, staffing, funding, and resource requirements of this law.

2. Within 60 days of the promulgation of this law, the Ministry of Counter Narcotics shall, in consultation with the Ministry of Public Health, prepare an organizational plan for the establishment of the Committee on Drug Control. Within 120 days of the promulgation of this Law, the Committee shall convene its inaugural meeting.

3. Within 120 days of the promulgation of this law, the Ministry for Counter Narcotics shall formulate and publish regulations pertaining to its activities and governance.

Article 58:

Entry into Force

This law shall enter into force from the date of its signing by the President and shall be published in the Official Gazette. Following the promulgation of this law, the Counter Narcotics Law published in the Official Gazette No. 813 dated 13.08.1383 shall be nullified.[50]

NOTES AND REFERENCES

1-Ahmad Ali Khalid. "Torture theology in the devil's republic." Daily Times, 4 March, 2011,

2--Muhammad Aftab. "Wanted: new policies to attract FDI." Daily Times, 7 March, 2011.

3--Rahimullah Yusufzai. "Persecuted for bravery." The News, 16 March, 2011.

4--Saulat Nagi. "The evil that men do." Daily Times, 28 March, 2011.

5--Shakeel Ahmad. "The growing menace of fake drugs." The Nation, 22 March, 2011.

6--Munazza Zuberi. "The Pakistani woman." Business Recorder, 12 March, 2011, Weekend. II

7--Musarrat Farooquei. "Women's rights to land and property." Business Recorder, 12 March, 2011.

8--Sikander Amani. "And then there were none." Daily Times, 7 March, 2011.

9--Syed Mansoor Hussain. "Punjab government and the young doctors." Daily Times, 21 March, 2011.

10--Syed Mansoor Hussain. "Why are young doctors so upset?." Daily Times, 7 March, 2011.

11--Yasser Latif Hamdani. "The way forward for the minorities of Pakistan." Daily Times, 7 March, 2011.

12--Zafar Azeem. "Trusts and beneficiary's rights to information." Business Recorder, 24 March, 2011.

13--Marschall, Ivonne. "Beware, the mercenaries ." Business Recorder, 16 March, 2011.

14--Mir Adnan Aziz. "Bondage with ease." The News, 30 March, 2011.

15--Nargis Khanum. "The costume of Sindh." Business Recorder, 19 March, 2011.

16-The sexually abused dancing boys of Afghanistan. By Rustam Qobil. BBC World Service.

17-Child abuse rife in Afghanistan: UN, Nov 23, 2009 9.

18--IRIN News, 20 January 2011.

19--Child sexual abuse cases increased in Afghanistan. by Muhammad Hassan Khitab on 22 November, 2010.

20--Guardian.co.uk. Jon Boone, Thursday 2 December 2010.

21--Cutting Edge. No Prosecutions for War Zone Sex Trafficking, Nick Schwellenbach and Carol D. Leonnig, July 26th 2010

22--Illicit weapon smuggling thrives in the North. Abdul Wahid Ahmad. Sunday, 20 February 2011

23- Sex Trade Thrives in Afghanistan. by Lisa Tang of the Associated Press, June 15, 2008.

24- Sex and security in Afghanistan. By David Isenberg. Asia Times, October 6, 2009.

25--Forced Marriages in Afghanistan. by Tahera Nassrat. 2011 Foreign Policy Blogs, Foreign Policy Association. April 6th, 2010.

26--Afghanistan: Marriage Practice Victimizes Young Girls, Society. Radiop Free Europe. January 04, 2008, By Farangis Najibullah.

27--Human Rights Watch (3 December 2009) "We Have the Promises of the World": Women's Rights in Afghanistan
...http://www.unhcr.org/refworld/pdfid/4b179c4a2.pdf

28--IRIN News (16 October 2007) Afghanistan: Widespread child marriage blamed for domestic violence http://www.irinnews.org/PrintReport.aspx?ReportID=74793.

29--Human Rights Watch interview with Rangina, May 6, 2009.

30--Human Rights Watch interview with Rangina, May 6, 2009.

31--Human Rights Watch interview with Rangina, May 6, 2009.

32--RAWA reported a 14-year-old Afghan girl, Samia, victim of gang-rape by Tajik warlords in Sar-e-Pul province in Northern Afghanistan. 2010.

33-- US Department of State report (2007) has placed Afghanistan as a source, transit, for women, and children trafficked for the purposes of commercial sexual exploitation.

34-- Afghanistan's Accidental Gay Pride. Nushin Arbabzadah. guardian.co.uk, Tuesday 24 May 2011.

35-- According to the State of the World's Mothers 2011 report, published on 24 June by NGO Save the Children, about 50 women die in childbirth each day in Afghanistan. One in three is physically or sexually abused and the average life expectancy of women is 44.

36-- An Interview with Malalai Joya (MP). The Harvard International Review, April 10, 2011). http://www.rawa.org/temp/runews/2011/04/10/malalai-joya-us-is-the-god-father-of-islamic-fundamentalism-in-the-region.html#ixzz1SpKh9yq8.

37-- Opium: a Shameful Phenomenon. By Jawad Rahmani. (Daily Outlook Afghanistan).

38-- On July 15, 2011, I came across a report of Pakistan's Federal Tax Ombudsman (January 2011) on the issue of ISAF's missing containers. This is a comprehensive report which gives readers a lot of information but only represents the Government of Pakistan's standpoint.

39-- In my telephone conversation with one of a senior advisor of Federal Tax Ombudsman in Islamabad. 2011.

40-- Daily Times (February 18, 2011), reported Pakistan's parliament Standing Committee serious reservations and pressure on Defence Minister and Chairman Federal Board of Revenue to explain the Government stance. The committee was told that only 7000 containers were missing which is not true. The Committee asked about the agreement between Pakistan and NATO Alliance which allowed the NATO-ISAF containers to pass through Pakistan without scrutiny.

41--Bacha Bazi: Afghan Tradition Expolits Young Boys: by Amanda Kloer • November 02, 2009.

42--Topics: Child Trafficking • Prostitution • Sex Trafficking: August 11, 2011.

43--Mothers are Still Vulnerable in Afghanistan: by Abdul Samad Haidari, Daily Outlook Afghanistan.

44--Afghan women fight back against harassment. In the first event of its kind, women in Afghanistan will march to raise awareness of street harassment. Noorjahan Akbar: 13 Jul 2011

45--The Plight of Afghan Children: August 15, 2011, by Sher Ali Yecha, Daily Outlook Afghanistan.

46--US Today, March 16, 2010.

47--Forced Marriages in Afghanistan: Los Angeles Times, April 3, 2002.

48--Kandahar's Lightly Veiled Homosexual Habits: Amnesty International (2005), Afghanistan: Women Still Under Attack – A Systematic Failure to Protect, ASA 11/007/2005, Amnesty International, London.

49--ECOSOC (United Nations Economic and Social Council) (2002), Discrimination against Women and Girls in Afghanistan: Report of the Secretary General, E/CN.6/2002/5, UN, New York.

50-- Missing Women and Bare Branches: Gender Balance and Conflict", Report, No. 11, The Woodrow Wilson International Center for Scholars, Washington, DC. Hudson, V. and A. Den Boer (2005).

51--The Status of Women in Afghanistan, HRW, New York, www.hrw.org. Human Rights Watch (2004).

52--A Dictionary of Islam, 1994 by T.P Hughes; Publisher Kazi Publications.

53--Al-Ghazali's Ihya' Ulum al-Din 1997; Translated by Dr. Ahmad A. Zidan; Islamic Inc. P.O. Box 1636, Cairo, Egypt.

Printed in Great Britain
by Amazon

86991185R00092